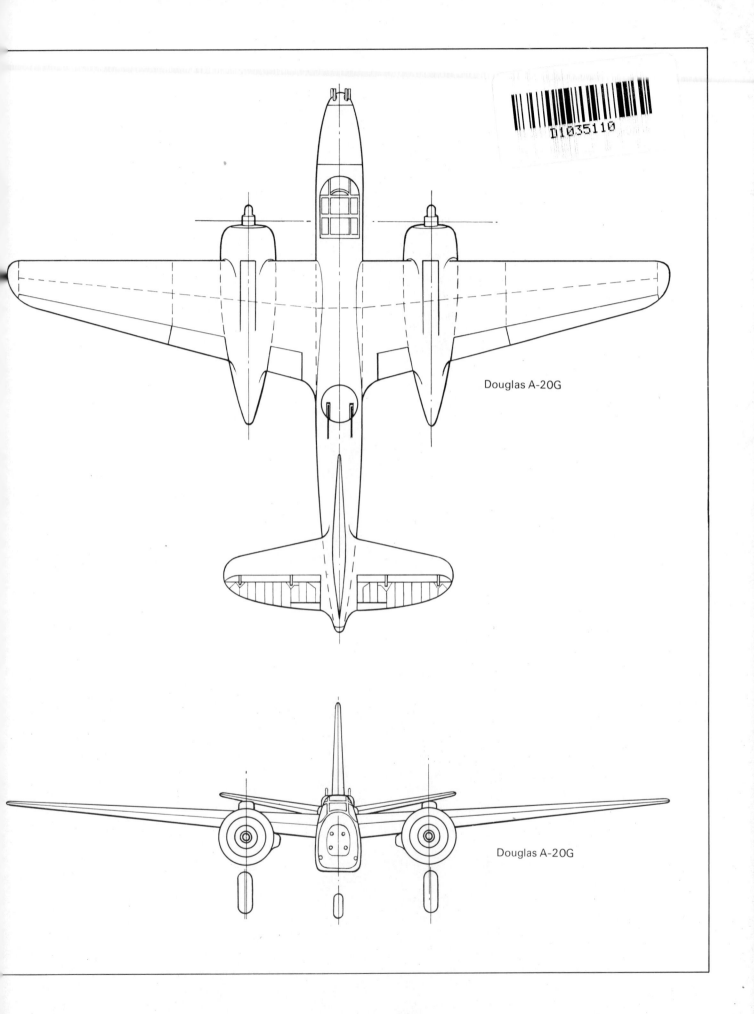

Douglas A-20G

Douglas A-20G

A-20 Havoc at War

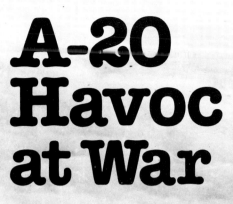

Below: Glass nosed A-20Js of the
9th Air Force. / *USAF*

Right: An A-20 of the 3rd Bomb Group flashes in on its bomb run over a Japanese freighter at Vigan. / USAF

A-20
Havoc
at War

Charles Scribner's Sons
NEW YORK

1 3 5 7 9 11 13 15 17 19 I/C 20 18 16 14 12 10 8 6 4 2

Printed in Great Britain

Library of Congress Catalog Card Number 79-54213
ISBN: 0-684-16453-1

Dedicated to
The Long Line of Men
Who took the Boston, the Havoc
and the Invader to War

Contents

Left: An A-20A of the 89th Squadron, 3rd Bomb
Group, following wheels up landing at Port Moresby,
New Guinea, in November 1942. / *USAF*

Introduction

The combat records of the Douglas A-20 Boston Havoc and the A-26 Invader stretch out over a period of 25 years and five major conflicts. There are very few sister aircraft whose record of missions and types of operations possess such diversification: any type of combat operation in any type of conflict – the Boston or Invader has performed it. Even the names and designations of the aircraft have undergone so many changes that they are often confusing: the Douglas A-20 is perhaps as well known as the Havoc, which was the designation the Americans used, as it was as the Boston. Shortly after World War II the US Air Force dropped the Attack prefix from its rolls and designated the Invader the B-26 rather than the A-26 and thus caused much bewilderment to those who remember the Martin B-26 Marauder of World War II fame.

As the Douglas DB-7, the Boston was one of the first American built aircraft to see action in World War II. It was initiated into combat over France with the French Air Force in 1940 and many Boston aircraft destined for France found their way to England and the Royal Air Force when the French surrendered.

The Royal Air Force was initially at a loss to find a mission and a purpose for the Boston. It found a niche first as an intruder aircraft, and renamed Havoc, but then many were taken over as 'Turbinlite' aircraft for night fighting duties. When this project was finally abandoned the Boston found its real role in North-West Europe. As a light bomber and tactical support aircraft it carried out an excellent job, not only with the Royal Air Force, but with the USAAF 9th Air Force flying from England and France.

In North Africa the Boston excelled not only with its original air crews, the South Africans, but later with the USAAF and the RAF. German airfields and harbour installations knew no rest with the Bostons in the air. The Boston then continued its tactical successes in the Mediterranean through the Sicilian and Italian campaigns.

The first A-20s arrived in the South-West Pacific when the USAAF was operating on a shoestring. Thanks to the genius of 'Pappy' Gunn, the forces there came up with a 'gunship' in the form of the A-20 that would strike fear into the hearts of the Japanese

throughout the fight up the coast of New Guinea and on to the Phillippines.

The A-26 Invader won its spurs in World War II as well. Faster, heavier and with greater armament and range, it was an immediate success in Northern Europe. Later it made many of the final strikes on the Japanese home islands destroying the enemy's aircraft and installations.

The end of World War II brought only a brief respite to the A-26 Invader. As the re-designated 'B-26' it returned to combat in Korea and compiled a tremendous record as an intruder and interdiction aircraft.

Further to the south the Invader went to combat in Indo-China in the conflict between the French and the Viet Minh. There it gave great support to French ground troops until the peace treaty which divided the country was signed.

The French made use of the Invader once more when they attempted to suppress the FLN insurgents in Algeria. However, there was little the Invader could really do in such a conflict even when relegated to the role of chasing hostile light aircraft by night.

The all-but-new 'On Mark' B-26s saw yeoman service with the USAF flying from Thailand, bombing and strafing along the Ho Chi Min trail, and the Invader performed in this capacity until near the end of the conflict in Vietnam.

To attempt to tell the entire story of these two aircraft is impossible. They have done too much. From night fighter, mine layer, Turbinlite fighter, low-level gunship, skip bomber, to counter-insurgency is a very, very long combat record. Many of the men who helped write this story have been most helpful and have taxed their memories to come up with the details of missions they flew as only they can relate. To these men my deepest thanks: Arthur Bird, Col Glenn W. Clark (Ret), Jean Cuny, Lt-Col Curtis R. Ehlert (Ret), Col Donald Hall (Ret), Charles Hinton, L. G. Holland, Col Milton W. Johnson (Ret), Lt-Col Tom Jones (Ret), L. M. King-Brewster, Paul Lambermont, Lt-Col Robert Mikesh (Ret), Jim Mansell, George McLannahan, A. J. Meshishnek, Donald F. Morrow, Aubrey Niner, Maj-Gen Nils Ohman (Ret), Russell L. Sturzebecker, Maj-Gen Frederick Terrell (Ret) and Charles V. Wilson.

The staff of the Simpson Historical Archives at Maxwell Air Force Base are to be cited once more for outstanding service in locating and making available those vital documents so necessary to any book of this type. To my fellow historians and others who helped so much with the photos and information my sincere appreciation: John Alcorn, Chaz Bowyer, CMS Robert Frink, Ed Furler, Bruce Hoy, Gregory Moreira, T/Sgt John Leibold, Lt-Col Charles Rush (Ret), Chris Shores, Frank Smith, Tom W. Stever, Norm Taylor and Kenn Rust who has always been my reliable helping hand. John Bardwell kept the prints coming again and had a lot to do with the final format of this book. Ann, Meg and Penny have suffered through another one. Bless'em all.

Houston, Texas　　　　*William N. Hess*

Below: One of three A-20As modified as an F-3 photo reconnaissance aircraft. The bomb bays were fitted with cameras and the armament was supplemented by a .30 calibre machine gun in the tail cone. / McDonnell Douglas

Birth of the Boston

As early as 1935 the Douglas Aircraft Company was aware of the coming need for a modern attack type aircraft that would replace the obsolete single engined craft of the day. They began development of a twin engined type that would carry a 1,000lb bomb load, have an impressive six machine gun armament installation and possess a top speed of 250mph.

While such a design was quite impressive at the time the even more rapid development of aircraft abroad soon dispelled thoughts of putting it into final production. When the US Army Air Corps formally announced a design competition in 1937 it was immediately apparent that a more advanced design would have to be laid out. Douglas came up with a twin engined aircraft powered by new Pratt & Whitney R-1830 engines rated at 1,100hp. The new prototype was a shoulder high monoplane with sleek lines and incorporated a tricycle landing gear. The craft could be manufactured with either a glass nose to house a bombardier or with a solid metal nose which could be fitted with multiple machine guns for low level strafing purposes. This aircraft, designated Douglas 7B, made its maiden flight on 26 October 1938, and immediately displayed qualities which were very condusive to the successes of the design that would follow.

As war clouds began to gather in Europe the French dispatched a purchasing commission to the United States in the hope that aircraft could be contracted and delivered before the shooting war became a reality. Strong isolationist factions in the United States made it most difficult for the French to negotiate with American aviation manufacturers, however, and all such dealings had to be kept under heavy wraps. The 'cat was really let out of the bag' on 23 January 1939. A member of the French commission was on a test flight aboard the Douglas 7B which was being flown by test pilot John Cable when it suffered a malfunction and crashed. Cable was killed in the crash but the passenger survived. The press soon discovered the 'mechanic' aboard was a member of the French purchasing commission. The unwanted publicity brought about a public apology from President Franklin Roosevelt and the public chastisement of US Air Corps General H. H. Arnold.

Regardless of US objections, however, the French placed an order for 105 DB-7s. The original order was later to be increased to 380. This design had been modified to an extent from the original 7B for better performance. The French version of the DB-7 still utilised the P & W R-1830 engine and was built in the glass nosed version. Instrumentation was on

Below: Predecessor to the DB-7 and A-20 was the Model 7B which looks more like an executive transport than an attack aircraft. / *McDonnell Douglas*

Top: The Douglas DB-7 which saw limited service in the Battle of France during 1940. This version of the aircraft was fitted with the Pratt & Whitney R-1830 engine. / *Via Cuny*

Above: The empenage of the DB-7 was tall and slender as shown in this photo of the aircraft during 1940. Its tricycle gear and split flaps made it an excellent aircraft for combat operations. / *Via Cuny*

Left: Twin .30 calibre machine guns comprised the rearward armament of the DB-7. Four .30 calibre guns were mounted on the fuselage sides for forward firing by the pilot. / *Via Cuny*

9

the metric system and armament was composed of four fixed 7.5mm Browning machine guns in the sides of the nose and had a bomb bay capacity of 1,800lb.

In August 1939 the US Army Air Corps let a contract for 63 of the DB-7s which were designated A-20. This was followed by a further order for 123 A-20As which were fitted with the Wright R-2600 Twin-Row Cyclone engine without supercharger whereas the American A-20 utilised a supercharged R-2600 power plant.

Great Britain contracted for 150 DB-7Bs in February of 1940. This model of the aircraft was pretty much as the American A-20, but with British equipment. May of 1940 and the German onslaught into France brought on a flood of orders from both France and Great Britain but the French had no time to use their aircraft to the full. The original intention had been to re-equip five Armée de L'air squadrons with DB-7s. When the German panzer divisions rolled into France only three French Escadrilles of DB-7s could be rushed to the front from North Africa where GB I/19, II/19 and II/61 had been re-equipping. The DB-7s were able to fly only some 70 or so sorties against the enemy, primarily against troops and panzer concentrations and did very little real damage. When the armistice came in June, eight or nine of the DB-7s had been lost in action and the balance had been flown back to North Africa. These surviving DB-7s became a part of the Vichy French Air Force in Morocco and Algeria during the period 1940-1942 and a number were destroyed on the ground by US Navy aircraft when the Americans invaded North Africa in November 1942. A number of other surviving DB-7s were later pressed into service in new Free French squadrons which resumed their fight against the Germans in North Africa in 1943.

Top: The Douglas A-20A, which was the original model ordered by the US Army Air Corps, was fitted with the Pratt & Whitney R-2600 engine and was a complete redesign of the Douglas DB-7, known as the DB-7B. / McDonnell Douglas

Above: A formation of USAAC A-20As in prewar olive drab and insignia. These new aircraft saw extensive operations in manoeuvres during the days just before America entered the war. / USAF

Left: The Douglas A-20C fitted with the bombardier nose differed from the DB-7B or Boston III primarily in a new exhaust system. It is readily recognised here by the individual exhaust stacks. / McDonnell Douglas

The A-20 in North-West Europe

The original British contract for the Douglas Boston was in the configuration of the American A-20 which was equipped with the Wright R-2600 engine and 150 of these aircraft were ordered February 1940. The first Bostons to arrive in England for service with the Royal Air Force, however, were the DB-7s which had been built for France. These aircraft began to arrive late in 1940 after the fall of France. They were powered by the Pratt & Whitney R-1830 engine and were completely equipped for French operations. The instruments were in French and metric, the radios were not compatible with the British system and the bomb bays would not take British bombs. Apart from this the primary shortcoming of the aircraft for use by the Royal Air Force was its lack of range. Its high speed and overall performance were an asset, but there was only one use they could find for the Boston I as it became known, and that was as a night fighter. The Boston I was rearmed with eight .30 calibre machine guns in the nose and assigned to No 23 Squadron. Following this initial assignment, a number of the aircraft were assigned to 'Turbinlite' squadrons for use as nocturnal interceptors and were fitted with 2,700 million candle-power searchlights in the nose. Another extraordinary job the Boston took on was that of dropping aerial mines in the path of incoming German raiders at night.

While the Bostons of No 23 Squadron did not meet with a great deal of success as night fighters, they did pioneer many of the night fighting tactics which were employed to better advantage when the later marks of the Beaufighter and the Mosquito came along. One operation in which the Boston I excelled while with No 23 Squadron was as a night intruder aircraft. The craft still maintained its capability of carrying 2,000lb of bombs and this coupled with its heavy machine gun armament made it an excellent aircraft in which to strike at German airfields on the Channel coast.

By late 1941 the Boston IIIs began to arrive in Britain. These aircraft were faster, had a longer range and were well received by the aircrews of the Royal Air Force from the beginning. The initial Boston IIIs were sent to Duxford for tactical testing and the first squadron to receive the aircraft was No 88 based at Attlebridge. Some of the pilots were dubious about the new craft, but an introductory flight was enough to convince most

Below: An in-flight shot of a Boston III showing the clean lines of the aircraft. While viewed suspiciously at the beginning by RAF pilots, it soon became a favourite in the squadrons who flew it. / IWM

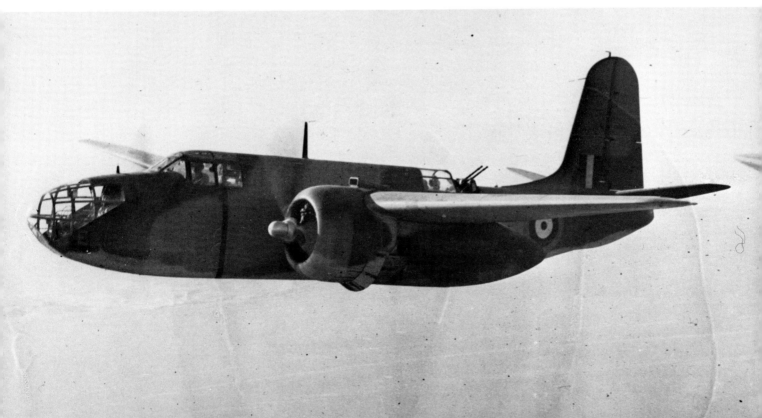

of them that they had a stable aircraft capable of an outstanding performance in any type of tactical operation.

No 226 Squadron at Wattisham began receiving Boston IIIs in October 1942 and by January 1943, No 107 Squadron became the third squadron to acquire the new aircraft. The first operational test came to the Boston IIIs on 12 February 1942, when their training routine was broken by the message that the German warships *Scharnhorst* and *Gneisenau* had left the harbour at Brest to dash through the Channel to safety in Germany.

Six Bostons of No 226 Squadron and four from No 88 Squadron were bombed up with 500lb bombs and took off in atrocious weather to seek the enemy. The crews from No 88 Squadron saw absolutely nothing and brought their bombs back home. One crew from No 226 Squadron made a momentary sighting through heavy cloud, but was unable to mount an attack.

Operations for the Boston squadrons got under way formally on 26 February 1942, when four aircraft from No 226 Squadron struck at shipping in the Channel. A small merchant vessel along with two flak ships were bombed with undetermined effect while one Boston suffered a hit in its engine and had its rear gunner wounded.

The spring of 1942 saw the Boston squadrons all become operational in earnest. While some low-level missions were flown it was found that the best altitude for Boston strikes was between 9,000 and 12,000ft. At this altitude the aircraft were too high for light flak which was deadly at low altitude and they were not above 14,000ft which was the point

12

Above left: A Boston III of No 107 Squadron RAF. This unit flew many of the early low-level missions over enemy-occupied territory. / IWM

Centre left: Boston III of No 107 Squadron. Note the Russian 'Hammer and Sickle' painted on the nose. Fairing for forward firing machine gun may be seen just below it. / IWM

Bottom left: No 107 Squadron RAF flying in echelon at medium altitude. The crews found that an altitude of 10,000-14,000ft was best suited for their operations. This way they were above the light flak and below the point where heavy flak was most effective. / IWM

Above: Bostons of No 342 'Lorraine' Squadron based in England. These Free French aircrews flew many missions against targets in their homeland. / Lambermont

at which heavy flak really became effective. However, the run in across the English Channel was usually flown below 2,000ft in order to cross the enemy coast with some degree of surprise.

The strikes by the Bostons were very heavily escorted by Royal Air Force Spitfires which were able to thwart most attacks by Luftwaffe fighters. These attacks which did get through necessitated one very important modification on the Boston. The blind spot under the tail brought about the installation of a .30 calibre machine gun that could be fired by a gunner through the bottom hatch.

The Bostons of No 2 Group Bomber Command, played a crucial role in the Dieppe commando operation which took place on 18 August 1942. At first light 10 Bostons from No 226 Squadron and two from other units went in to drop smoke bombs to blind the German gun batteries on the eastern cliffs. The Bostons came in right on the deck and discharged their loads, placing 150 of the 100lb projectiles on the target area. The smoke set off by the bombs left a screen some 800-1,000yd long which was promptly picked up by the wind and carried some four to five miles out to sea giving the invaders excellent cover. To accomplish their mission the men of the Bostons had braved intense and accurate flak so effective that nine of the 12 aircraft were damaged, two so severely that they made crash landings at Middle Wallop.

All day Bostons from No 2 Group struck at enemy gun batteries and installations in support of the ground troops. Heavy flak was encountered on all missions and six Bostons

from No 88 Squadrons encountered 20 Fw190s on one of their missions. The Bostons turned into the enemy formation and corkscrewed down to their target but all their bombs missed. All the Bostons were damaged by enemy fire, one so badly that it had to ditch in the Channel.

Five crews from No 226 Squadron flew the final mission of the day, braving intense fire from the enemy cliffs in order to lay their smoke right down over the water in order to cover the withdrawal of the commando operation. Eleven low-level runs were made in rapidly deteriorating weather. One Boston went down into the sea and only one made it back to its home base. The rest put down at the first airfield they could find.

Another outstanding operation in the annals of Boston operations in North-West Europe is the mission of 6 December 1942, when the three Boston squadrons, along with Ventura and Mosquito squadrons, struck the Phillips radio and radar equipment manufacturing plant at Eindhoven, Holland. On that day the Bostons hugged the deck all the way, fought off determined attacks by German fighters and flew through intense flak to put their bombs on the target. Excellent results were obtained and four of the Bostons were downed, three of them falling to German fighters.

During spring 1943, No 342 Free French 'Lorraine' Squadron was equipped with Bostons. They were soon flying missions with the other Boston-equipped squadrons; sometimes medium altitude strikes and at other times they attacked airfields, power stations and the like at treetop level. One historic

Far left: A-20Gs of the USAAF's
410th Bombardment Group return
from a strike against targets in
France. Heavy anti-aircraft
installations kept most A-20 strikes
at medium altitude in North-West
Europe. / USAAF

Left: Combat and tragedy go hand
in hand. Here an American A-20
has just burst into flames after
taking a direct hit from a German
flak battery. / USAF

Below: Boston IIIs of No 88
Squadron RAF make ready to take
off on their smokescreen laying
mission on D-Day, 6 June 1944.
Note the invasion stripes that have
just been painted on. The white
noses were not used on most
aircraft that day. / IWM

Above: A formation of 9th Air Force A-20s. Glass-nosed A-20Js leading the formations were used to provide the bombardier for the gun-nosed A-20Gs. / *USAF*

mission for the 'Lorraine' Squadron took place on 3 October 1943. On this date 12 Bostons were briefed to attack Chevilly Larue, an electrical power station near Orly airfield in Paris. For many of the French aircrew it would be a trip home for the first time since 1940.

At 1248 hours 12 aircraft under the command of Col Rancourt were airborne. Visibility was excellent and the Bostons raced across the Channel and over the French coast right on the deck. The planes flew so low that bicycling children sought shelter in the ditches along the road. As they neared Saint-Remy de Chevreuse, still unmolested, the Bostons began to climb to 1,500ft for bombing.

Bomb bay doors came open and the Frenchmen dropped their bomb loads on the target with excellent results. However, many of them could not resist the chance to call out familiar landmarks to each other over the intercom and one or two even sighted their homes as they flashed over the city of Paris.

The Boston flown by Lt Lamy was hit and to avoid crashing into a residential section of the city the pilot managed to put it down in the River Seine. Two crew members died, but it was reported later that one had survived. The aircraft flown by Lt Lucchesi was hit in one engine and limped away from the target area and reached the area of Compiegne

where the pilot managed to crash land. Lucchesi was able to evade the enemy and finally got back to England. Pilots of No 342 Squadron would later be remembered for the excellent job they did laying smoke-screens for the invading ground forces on D-Day in Normandy, 6 June 1944.

Both No 88 and No 342 Squadrons continued to fly tactical missions in Boston IIIs and IVs until the end of World War II. No 266 Squadron gave up its Bostons in 1943 for North American Mitchells and No 107 Squadron received Mosquitos early in 1944.

The first Douglas A-20 missions by the United States Army Air Forces were flown by the 15th Bombardment Squadron in July 1942, but this unit was destined to journey on to North Africa in the autumn of that year. It was not until the spring of 1944 that the three A-20 units of the 9th Air Force arrived and began to fly missions from England. These units were the 409th, 410th and 416th Bombardment Groups.

The A-20s that went into action with these units were J and G models. The glass-nosed Js carried bombardiers and were used to lead the formations in their bombing which was carried out at altitudes ranging from 10,000 to 14,000ft. Each of the groups had four assigned squadrons and usually each squadron dispatched six aircraft on a combat mission. More often than not, the A-20s had individual

targets assigned to each squadron. The lead aircraft and the deputy lead aircraft were glass-nosed models carrying bombardiers. The balance were solid-nosed gun-armed aircraft who salvoed their bombs on signal from the lead plane.

At the time the 9th Air Force 'Havocs', as the Americans decided to call the A-20, went into action the Germans were beginning their V-1 rocket campaign against England in earnest. These missiles were launched from long ski-like ramps and were scattered along the coast of France. The A-20s were put into action immediately against these targets on what were called 'No Ball' missions. The speed of the A-20 and the accuracy of the Norden bombsight made the Havocs particularly effective in the destruction of these pin-point and well-defended sites.

Late May and early June 1944 brought about the final interdiction missions against German installations along the French coast in preparation for the invasion on 6 June. The A-20s were put to work striking at bridges, railroad marshalling yards and all types of primary road targets to cut the transportation lanes to the Cherbourg Peninsula.

On 6 June the A-20s faced the heaviest flak opposition that they had ever encountered in striking coastal gun batteries along the invasion coast. Regardless of their losses the A-20 crews all got in at least two missions in support of the ground forces that day. Most targets were destroyed by their accurate bombing and the crews were most jubilant that evening to learn that the ground forces had established their beachheads and were on the Continent to stay. Their interdiction missions took on a more real and important meaning now that the troops were ashore and depending on airpower to help in the advance.

Throughout the month of June the A-20s continued to strike at transportation and communications targets in France to aid the advancing infantrymen who were having a hard time smashing through the hedgerows of the difficult bocage country. By early July the Havocs and Martin B-26 Marauders of the 9th Air Force had destroyed the bridges over the River Seine and wrecked most of those across the Loire. As the Germans made frantic attempts to repair the bridges the American bombers struck again and again at the rail centres and bridges that were still in use.

On the morning of 6 August 1944 the 416th Bomb Group took off to strike Oissel Bridge, one of the few remaining across the River Seine. Upon approaching the target the formation was blocked by a weather front that had moved in, so they returned to base with their bombs.

Undoubtedly, this alerted the enemy for when the formation returned late in the

Above and right: And then came winter. By autumn 1944 most of the 9th Air Force A-20 units were in France. These aircraft did yeoman duty during Europe's worst winter in many years, particularly during the 'Battle of the Bulge'. These pictures portray the conditions under which they had to operate. Their success was a real credit to the men on the ground who kept them airborne and to the air crews who braved the elements. / USAF

evening the enemy was waiting for them. Gun emplacements extended on each side of the river for miles. The intense flak barrage greeted them at the beginning of their bomb run and stayed with them throughout their rally off the target. Four of the A-20s failed to return to base that evening and of those that got home practically all had suffered extensive flak damage. Regardless, the men of the 416th had put their bombs right on the target and another vital bridge had been denied to the Germans.

Two days later the 416th again braved intense flak to destroy the rail junction at Frevant. Two A-20s went down over the target but at least half of the large rail repair shop was destroyed as well as several other smaller installations surrounding it. As the formation headed for home it was attacked by a flight of four Messerschmitt Bf109s, but escorting P-38s managed to break up the attack before the Germans could get at the Havocs.

By November 1944 the new Douglas A-26 Invaders began to arrive on the scene with the 9th Bomber Command. First to get them

was the veteran 416th Bomb Group which along with the 409th and 410th Bomb Groups was now operational on an advanced field in France. It was left to the 410th Group to carry on with full scale operations in the A-20.

It was the 410th that was called on to do yeoman duty in December 1944 when German panzer columns broke through the American lines in the 'Battle of the Bulge'. In the five-day period from 23 December 1944 the 410th Group dropped 1,768 500lb bombs on targets throughout the breakthrough area. Tired air crews flew mission after mission against Von Rundstedt's armoured columns and most of their bombs found the target. The tireless ground crews worked throughout the night to have the A-20s ready to fly in support of the beleagured American ground forces each morning. For their efforts the men of the 410th were awarded a Distinguished Unit Citation.

In February 1945 the 410th Group began flying night missions. Martin B-26s and Douglas A-26 Invaders were used as path-finder aircraft to illuminate the targets and the A-20s of the 410th then came in to bomb. Bombing was done in sections of three with the aircraft vertically separated by 100ft intervals. With practice the hitherto 'day bomber' A-20 pilots became highly proficient in the dark.

The A-20s of the 410th flew against enemy targets right up to the end of the war, although they had started to re-equip with A-26s when the European war came to an end. The versatile A-20 had led the Germans a miserable life from a tactical standpoint. From the initiation of the first Boston of the RAF up until the end with Havocs, no bridges, rolling stock, marshalling yards or tactical target escaped their bombs. Theirs was one of the outstanding achievements in the air war over North-West Europe.

Left: An A-20 in Russian markings landing at Ladd Field, Alaska. / McDonnell Douglas

Below: Toward the end of the war in Europe some of the A-20 squadrons of the 9th Air Force began flying night missions. Here Helen 7X-T of the 410th Bomb Group gets airborne. / USAF

While little can be learned of their combat operations, some 3,125 A-20s went to Russia. It is known that they did creditable service at the Battle of Stalingrad and were well liked by the Russians for ground support duties. These photos were made at Ladd Field, Alaska, where the A-20s in Russian markings were turned over to ferry pilots who took them on into their homeland in the USSR.
/ USAF

Turbinlite Operations
L. M. King-Brewster

'Early experiments were made on searchlights in aircraft in World War I using a filament lamp rated at 3kW. Early in 1940 a further investigation was made on the possible use of high power airborne searchlights, but the matter was apparently dropped. In October 1940 the Research Laboratories of the General Electric Company of England were approached by the late Air-Cdre W. Helmore of the Ministry of Aircraft Production and asked to co-operate in a new development which included the concept of an illuminating aircraft operating with separate fighters. This was the birth of the Tubinlite, although it was originally called Air Target Illumination (ATI). Its main function was to help night interceptions using the primitive Air Interception (AI) radar of the day which had a minimum range well in excess of normal night-time visibility. My boss at the Laboratories was then the late L. B. W. Jolley who had been concerned with both of the previous projects. He was also closely concerned with turbines, hence

the codename Turbinlite, usually referred to as the Helmore Turbinelite.

'At this time, the late Wg Cdr F. S. Cotton was concerned jointly with Helmore in the direction of the project. However, for practical purposes I would regard Helmore as the originator of the project, with electrical design, development and co-ordination by GEC to his overall requirements. Similarly all aircraft modifications and design were under L. E. Baynes, chief designer of Alan Muntz Ltd, also to Helmore's requirements.

'From my limited information I believe that the DB-7 or Havoc was chosen for the following reasons:

Below: The Royal Air Force employed the first Boston IIs and some IIIs as Turbinlite versions of the night fighter they called the Havoc II. These aircraft carried a 2,700 million candlepower searchlight in the nose. / *IWM*

1 Availability
2 It could carry a relatively bulky power source and equipment weighing 2,000/3,000lb
3 It could be modified to carry a large mirror on the nose
4 It possessed the necessary speed and manoeuvrability to deal with the enemy bomber targets of the time.

'Most of the flight development was done by a special experimental night fighter equipment flight of the Ministry of Aircraft Production (MAP) (1422 Flight) at Heston aerodrome under the command of Wg Cdr A. E. Clouston (later Air-Cdre CB, DSO, DFC, AFC and Bar). The first 16 aircraft were either Havoc I or II, and were fitted out at Heston. The 16 were completed by end July 1941, just nine months from the start of lamp development. Three Boston IIIs were fitted at Heston shortly afterwards. The remainder of all types were fitted and modified at the Burton-wood Repair Depot. I believe that the total number of aircraft including those from Heston approached 100. Flights were eventually deployed at some six airfields throughout England.

'According to Clouston handling of the aircraft was virtually unaltered and that the extra drag and speed reduction due to the flat nose were very small due to the use of the Townend Ring as suggested by Baynes. The fact that the handling was still very good appears confirmed by the spectacular manner in which Clouston and other Heston pilots threw the aircraft around.

'The light in the nose had as its power supply four banks of 12 special 12V 35A/hr lead-acid accumulators, two banks in each half of the bomb bay. These were charged on the ground from an external source, with special provision for forced ventilation to prevent any build-up of hydrogen. Battery weight was approximately 1,920lb.

'The Turbinlite aircraft was accompanied by two Hawker Hurricane single seat fighter aircraft, one flying off each wing. The Turbinlite pilot was supposed to get the target in azimuth near either edge of the beam (width ± 15°) so that in theory return fire aimed at the light source should pass behind his aircraft. He would see no direct light from the Turbinlite, and at altitude back-scatter should not be too serious in the absence of cloud or high altitude haze. Note that the outer fighter pilot was in a much better position to see the target because of his large offset from the beam, and could on occasion see a target in or against the beam even when the Turbinlite pilot could not.

'Station keeping was achieved by the use of special illuminated strips on the upper and lower wing surfaces of the Havoc, the former for the fighter above and the latter for the fighter below.

'A white strip having special characteristics was provided on each wing surface and illuminated by small projectors mounted high in the fuselage for the upper surfaces and in the engine nacelles for the lower. The optics were such that the light could pass out through a small hole in the aircraft skin, and almost no light could be seen outside other than off the white strips. The light intensity was under the control of the Havoc pilot.

Above: An RAF Havoc II clearly showing the searchlight installation fitted to the Turbinlite flights. / *King-Brewster*

Right: Nose of the Havoc II showing searchlight shutters open and closed. The shutter allowed the light to build up to full intensity before opening. When switched off the shutter prevented the aircraft from being seen from the gleam of red hot carbons. / *King-Brewster*

Far right, top: Pilot's controls for station keeping lights which enabled the fighters to keep their position. / *King-Brewster*

Far right, bottom: A flight of Havoc II Turbinlite aircraft. Note the station-keeping strips on the trailing edge of the wings. / *King-Brewster*

26

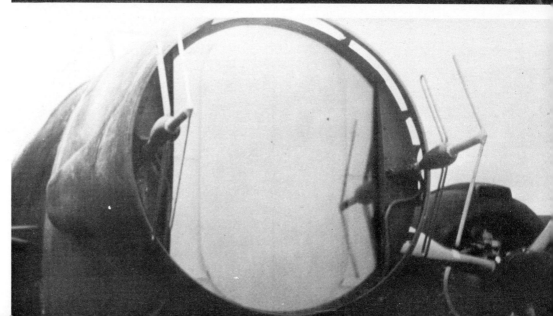

'To get into formation, maximum light intensity was used sometimes assisted initially by the navigation lights or radar. When the fighter was in position above/below the Turbinlite and 200-300yd behind, the Turbinlite pilot would reduce the light intensity to the minimum required by the fighter to maintain station. There were obvious problems in the presence of cloud or poor visibility. One technique for transit through cloud was to send the fighter ahead, with the Turbinlite aircraft following by means of its own radar.

'Much effort was expended on the Turbinlite from the time of its inception in the early days of the blitz, but in the course of time it never achieved much identified success apart from its possible value as a deterrent. By the time it was adequately deployed, the blitz against the cities of England had reduced, the minimum range of the AI radar which it was intended to assist had improved, and the speed and altitude of the enemy bombers had increased. There is little doubt, however, that had sufficient numbers of these aircraft been available during the blitz of 1940-1941 it is highly probable that the story would have been different.'

Turbinlite Pilot

One of those pilots who knew the frustration of Turbinlite missions was L. G. Holland who found himself assigned to No 534 Squadron based at Tangmere during summer 1942.

'If memory serves me right there were Turbinlite Units at Predannock in Cornwall, Tangmere, West Malling or somewhere else in Kent, Hunsdon, Acklington near Newcastle upon Tyne, and another possibly further north in Scotland at Turnhouse or Drem.

'No 534 Squadron had a mixture of Havoc and Boston I, II and IIIs. They all carried the same equipment – a searchlight in the nose behind a flat glass disc and a pair of doors, and a belly full of very heavy batteries though I only recall one case of them falling out due to abnormal loading. The nose was surrounded by a Townend ring. The aircraft were also equipped with AI MkIV but carried no armament. One or two Hurricane IIc (four 20mm cannon) flew in formation on a pair of diminutive station-keeping lights. Most of the Hurricane pilots preferred to rely on the Havoc exhaust. How they kept station in the filthiest weather at night I have never understood and I never heard of a collision despite the abrupt manoeuvre demanded by the radar operators.

'The function of this "weapons system" was of course to track and close on a target using ground control and AI or the searchlight "box". Having closed to about 400yd, the searchlight arc was struck but the doors kept closed and the attendant Hurricane given a code word – "Boiling" or some such – drew ahead. After a few seconds the light was exposed, supposedly pinning the victim in the beam light right in front of the fighters. It was a very bright light and most embarrassing for anyone caught in it, especially if they were unwise enough to look towards it. The "searchlight box" depended on ground searchlights only being exposed within a map reference square over which the target was passing, attempting at the same time to illuminate it and indicate its direction. In this latter they were rarely successful but the general indication was as good as ground control except for altitude information. The "box" was, of course, used with all forms of night fighter and probably contributed to many successful interceptions.

'In the latter half of 1942 enemy targets were few and far between and what we called "straight" night fighters using AI MkIV, V, VI and VII were always given the "scramble" targets. As far as I know, no enemy aircraft was destroyed by a Turbinlite team and at the end of 1942 when all units were disbanded, the lights were fitted on Wellingtons, Warwicks, Catalinas and perhaps, Liberators for anti-submarine patrols over the Bay of Biscay.

'To return to the DB-7 or Havoc. It was a popular aircraft despite its permanent deadweight of a Turbinlite. While the "straight" night fighter squadrons and intruder squadrons enjoyed a good measure of success in the Havoc and Boston; we of the Turbinlite Squadrons could claim was that we formed a few bricks in the defensive wall and that we learned much through flying in close company with other aircraft in all weather at night.'

Mine Laying Havoc

George McLannahan

'I joined No 93 Squadron at Middle Wallop on 23 December 1940. The CO, Wg Cdr John Homer, informed me on arrival that we were a mine laying squadron and this was something of a shock to me as I had volunteered for night fighters! It was, however, aerial mine laying and it was carried out by Handley Page Harrows patrolling at around 20,000ft. They carried about 120 aerial mines and laid them in a line approximately one mile long and extending to a depth of 2,000ft. Once the bomb bay doors were opened and the switch operated to release the first mine, the remainder followed automatically one at a time. The device itself was contained in a canister, which was around 10-12in long and 6-8in in diameter.

'This canister contained a 36in parachute which deployed on release and 2,000ft of "piano" wire. Attached to the end of the wire was a one pound bomb with a circular wheel-like striker pin at the top and below it a small stablilising parachute. The theory was that aircraft flying into one of more of these wires would continue until the larger parachute had pulled the mine up to contact the wing of the aircraft. The small stabiliser parachute was not deployed until the wire was struck.

'To operate the device the aircraft was vectored by a Ground Control Interception (GCI) station into a position above, ahead and to one side of the target. When in position the bomb doors were opened and on the GCI controller's instructions the aircraft was turned across the target's path and the mines were released.

'At the time I joined it, the squadron was receiving a few Havocs and I did my first solo in one on 8 January 1941. We had three at that time; AW411, BD110 and BD117. We later received some DB-7s. These DB-7s were originally intended for the French Air Force and possessed no armament. Their instrumentation was very foreign to us as the air speed indicator was in kilometres per hour and the boost gauges registered in PZs. We normally took-off at full throttle which, as they had no boost control, tended to overboost. Being empty and very light the aircraft leapt off the ground and my recollection of my first take-off was that I was throttling back at about 500ft to keep out of cloud while I retracted the undercarriage. I hadn't anticipated the low cloud base and I then realised that I'd left my sector map at dispersal. It was then that I really appreciated the DB-7's beautiful handling as I was circling the countryside at about 400ft with the side window open looking for familiar landmarks. The aircraft more or less flew itself whilst I found my bearings and followed the Andover road back to Middle Wallop.

'I flew my first "Mutton" (mine laying) mission from Middle Wallop on 15 April 1941, the second and third were from Exeter where we positioned for control in the Plymouth area with Axminster GCI. The third took place on 29 April, lasted 1hr 45min and I landed back at Middle Wallop having released my mines somewhere off Start Point. We always operated over the sea because of the danger of our load hitting someone on the ground. The mines were supposed to be self destroying before reaching ground level but miles of wire would be very awkward wherever it arrived on land. Although I didn't see it, I believe one Harrow, in the early days returned minus most of its fabric fuselage cover due to its load self destructing too soon after release.

'My patrol notes for the 29 April mission read: "After I fired the mines off on this night above some cloud there was a series of explosions below and behind us. They continued intermittently for a period and gave the impression that at any rate the Hun had jettisoned his bombs. We returned to Middle Wallop and reported the night's happenings." Later that night a report came in from a coastguard that an aircraft had crashed on land about 15-20min after I had let the mines go. This crash was never found, but somehow or other it was recorded that the enemy was destroyed and I was credited with it.

'I'm afraid we had little or no confidence in the long aerial mine. "Mutton" was conceived to combat the bomber stream but by the time it was perfected the stream had been broken up by other means and "Mutton" had to try and operate against single targets.'

Low-Level Operations – North-West Europe Tactics

Flt Lt R. A. Yates-Earle

'There are two forms of low-level attack, one of a limited scope where a few aircraft attack a small target, the other a full-scale assault by several squadrons or even a whole group.

'Sometimes our A-20s had special missions to perform, such as the time we were called upon to lay smoke from low level to screen the commando raid on Dieppe. They wanted the smoke laid in front of the coastal batteries, from which they were expecting some trouble. We went in over the north beach and dropped 100lb phosphorous bombs, which produce a lot of smoke. Then we flew on around behind the town and out over the south beach. I was impressed by the depth to which the German's defences extended; there wasn't any time during the whole trip that they weren't shooting at me with some sort of light machine gun. The whole Channel coast was really well defended.

'We made several more sorties, laying smoke first by 100lb phosphorous bombs, and later by spray from containers so that it came out in a cloud behind the aircraft. This is not nearly as good a way of laying smoke as from phosphorous bombs, because you had to fly straight and level and couldn't take any evasive action.

'A typical large-scale action at low level was an attack we made on the large Phillips radio works at Eindhoven in Holland. We went in between Dunkirk and Ostend, hit the target and came out over The Hague. The type of formation we used for jobs like that was waves of eight airplanes flying in a loose echelon. It is not formation flying at all; it is more or less follow the leader in groups. And we flew along widely separated so that each aircraft could take individual evasive action.

'All we had to bother about really was light flak. If there is a gun firing at you from the

Below: A Boston III from No 88 Squadron making a low-level run over England. The early Boston units soon learned that the aircraft had a blind spot beneath the tail. This was resolved by adding a .30 calibre gun firing out of a ventral hatch. / *IWM*

left or right, you can see the tracer coming up to you, and the best way to dodge that was to make a sort of porpoising motion. (Of course, if you could, you tried to put an obstacle between you and the flak gunner in the form of a tree or haystack; he lost sight of you for a moment and by the time he got a bead on you again you were miles away.) If, on the other hand, he was shooting at you from the front, the best thing to do was go straight for him and he would have to put his head down. The four forward-firing guns on the Boston and the fact that even if he hit you it would probably bring the aircraft crashing down on him caused him to duck.

'In the Eindhoven raid we had our first eight aircraft go in at low level all the way, dropping delay bombs that had an 11-second fuse. The following waves, carrying 500lb medium-case bombs with instantaneous fuses, climbed to 1,500ft about two miles from the target, dropped them, dived down to deck level and went on out.

'Things went a bit wrong on that mission after leaving the target. The leading observer made a slight mistake and took us out over the Hook of Holland. The Hook was very heavily defended and when we got there we saw hundreds of Germans dashing out of huts and rushing up to their gun emplacements. We had very good sport shooting them with our front guns, but when we got out to sea they got their wind back and fired at us with damm big coastal guns. They didn't do much damage to us, but it looked pretty unpleasant for a while.

'When you made a low-level attack with a small formation (about three aircraft) you wanted fighter escort all the way, instead of just meeting you on the way out as at Eindhoven, or else you wanted cloud cover.

'On "rhubarb" (ground strafing) missions the navigation wasn't important. We flew very short range and our job was to attack any target we could find. We would just go looking for trains, truck convoys, etc. As soon as we got to the target area, we were in communication with the base.

'But if you were leading a formation of, say, 70 aircraft, as at Eindhoven, flying below treetop level most of the time, it was extremely difficult to trace your way and find one small factory in all that country. In fact, the only way to do it, even with an observer, was to make a point of hitting some railway or canal or roadway that would lead you to the target. And if you did get lost you certainly couldn't make circuits with 70 aircraft behind you. If you missed the target the first time, that was it. You went home.

'In attacking a large target, you tightened up while making the bombing run and bombed in line abreast; or if it was a small target, not more than three aircraft went over in line astern. Once you got to the target you closed up and everybody took his own target. If you were attacking a big factory, with maybe dozens of buildings, you studied them and assigned specific aircraft to specific targets. The whole object of low-level missions was to drop bombs dead on the spot.'

Below: Boston IIIs of No 88 Squadron RAF. This squadron flew many strikes against the occupied coasts and laid the smokescreens to cover the commando raid on Dieppe on 19 August 1942. / *IWM*

Operations

Jim Mansell

'During my time with No 88 Squadron as an air gunner/radio operator our Boston IIIs were used exclusively for daylight operations of various kinds. There was the circus operation, the low-level formation, and the low-level individual or intruder type of operation. The circus operation was devised to replace the large fighter sweeps which had failed to entice the enemy fighters off the ground. It was thought that a force of medium bombers attacking key targets such as docks, airfields, factories would force the German fighters to engage, thereby giving our Spitfire escort a crack at them.

'The usual procedure was for the Boston squadron, 12 aircraft in two boxes of six in double vic formation, after rendezvous on the English Channel coast with the Spitfire fighter wing, to fly across the Channel at around 50ft to beat the German radar. At about 10 minutes to the target, we climbed, aiming to be at 12,000ft for the attack. In addition to the close escort we had medium cover and top cover – all Spitfires. All aircraft took the bombing cue from the leader. As is well known, the hottest opposition from flak and fighters came on the run-in, especially the straight and level bombing run. After bombing the formation went into a steep diving turn, usually to port, losing about 6,000ft very quickly and coming out of the dive going like "bats out of hell". Some of the circuses in which I took part were attacks on Le Harve, St Malo, Flushing, Brest, Abbeville and St Omer. For this type of operation the usual crew of three became a crew of four with the addition of an air gunner. The German fighters had learned quickly that the Boston was vulnerable under the tail. Because of the upswept tailplane and the large fin and rudder it was not possible to bring the top guns to bear on a fighter climbing straight up under the tail. Accordingly, another gun position was improvised. A single bar mounting which carried a Vickers gas operated machine gun could be swung down across the rear escape hatch. The air gunner then lay on the floor of the aircraft, head towards the rear, and fired at any enemy fighter coming up under the tail.

By using all tracer, it became a very useful scare-gun.

'One memorable circus for me took place on 21 January 1943. The target was the docks at Flushing and after morning briefing we took off at 1400 hours. It seemed straight-forward enough – two boxes of six aircraft in line astern going inland first and after a turn to port of 180 degrees, attacking the target on the way out to sea, at about 12,000ft. We were flying number three in the second box, on the leader's port side. It so happened that the leader of the second box was inexperienced in spite of his senior rank, and on the turn to port just before the attack he overshot the leading box, which resulted in our box having to make a steep turn to port to avoid a collision. Since we were on the inside of the turn we found ourselves standing on our port wingtip with the inevitable result – a high speed stall. Within seconds our Boston was plummetting for the middle of Flushing harbour. Since there was a fair amount of flak about I thought my pilot, Flt Sgt Jack Wilson, had been hit and we were out of control. He was too busy to use the intercom just then. He regained control quickly but continued to dive steeply in order to avoid the light flak that was coming at us. Of course, I didn't realise this and was struggling to get my chute pack which was stowed on the side of the aircraft. I had it on and had my hand on the ripcord ready to go headfirst through the open hatch when good old "O for Orange" pulled out of the dive and screamed out of the harbour at 1,000ft and 350mph plus. I must admit it was one of my worst moments.

'Another shaky "do" was a low-level attack on an airfield. On 1 November 1942, we were reserve crew on the battle order when we were called to a morning briefing. Someone had dreamed up a new type of operation. It was a low-level attack by a box of six aircraft in loose formation – two vics of three. We learned at the briefing that the formation was to fly at low level across the Channel, crossing the French coast at a point roughly midway between Calais and Wissant. Since the enemy defences were strong here, they were to be attacked by several squadrons of Spitfires literally seconds before the bombers were due to cross. This would keep the German's heads down and make the passage easier. Approaching the airfield at St Omer the formation would climb to 800ft that being the safety height for the bomb load which was 40-pounders. This struck fear into the hearts of aircrew. At that time they were the only bombs without a safety device. And 800ft was a height at which aircraft were beginning to look slow to the ground gunners, which made them very vulnerable indeed. The formation was to take the bombing cue from the leader, thereby causing the kind of "blanket bombing" of the target which could do the most damage. After bombing, a swoop down to low level and sneak out the way we came in.

'Well, to say the CO's "gen" was unpopular was a remarkable understatement. It wasn't the kind of trip to look forward to, and we, that is Wilson's crew in Boston "O for Orange" were very thankful we were reserve aircraft. Our job was to "tail" the formation as far as the English coast, just in the un-likely event of mechanical failure in the other aircraft. Then it was a sharp turn round and back to base.

'As we walked out to the crew bus we commiserated with our close "oppo's", Ray New and his crew. Ray, an American from Kentucky who joined the RAF in 1940, was flying number two. Take-off was at 1300 hours and we were soon flying south at low level about 400yd behind the formation. Then the unlikely event occurred. Ray New pulled out of formation dragging smoke from the port engine, and Jack Wilson, with a few well chosen words on the intercom, pushed the throttle open to ease up into his place. Nothing very much was said as we left the English coast and wave hopped across the Channel. Guns were tested and we settled down for the run-in. As we approached the dunes of the French coast there was no sign of the Spitfires – everthing looked quiet. The second vic of three following instruction, had eased back a distance of 70-80yd behind the first vic in which we were flying. As we closed in towards the beach all hell was let loose. We were flying into a dense screen of tracer. There was no room nor time for evasive action. We just hammered on through it. As we cleared the worst of it I saw our number 5, a young pilot officer called Hulme, caught in a hail of light stuff. Suddenly, the Boston's nose went up until it was silhouetted against the sky at about 300ft then it went on its back and plunged, with a violent ex-plosion, into the ground. The crew had no chance. We had been hit, too, but there was no serious damage; at least there didn't appear to be since we kept flying. I was feeling sick about the crew who'd "bought it"

but the ground gunners gave us no time to dwell on it. I looked across at the CO, Wg Cdr Pelly-Fry. There was a hole in the side of the Boston just aft of the gunner's seat. There was a fire and some of the ammo in the pans used for the scare gun had been set off. I wondered if the gunner "Buster" Evans had been hit and then I saw him through a hole in the fuselage. He was on his knees, beating out the fire with his gloves. He saw me looking and read the unspoken question. His answer was a broad grin and the thumbs up sign. "Buster" was a real operational type.

'We had reached the point, almost in sight of the airfield, when we had to begin the climb to 800ft. The CO's nose went up, Jack Wilson said "Going up", and the real job had begun. We made one bombing run but the old man wasn't satisfied and we had to go round again, making a wide sweep to line up on the target as before, still at 800ft. Well, the first run had been bad enough, but the second was unbelievable. I stole a glance ahead as we approached the perimeter and remember thinking, "This is it, we can't possibly survive in that." The light flak and machine gun fire was so thick it seemed impenetrable. But we did survive, mira-culously. I heard Mac's "Bombs gone", felt the lift, and then the formation had exploded to all points of the compass. We turned sharply to starboard, heading inland before making a sweep round, to get on course for home. Fortunately, no fighters appeared, and as we approached the coast, roughly at the point of entry, we joined up with a Boston flown by Doug Smith, another New Zea-lander. This time we were prepared and the two Bostons, flying abreast, dived on the coast defence and opened up with the front guns. As we shot out over the sea, I fired to cover Doug Smith's tail, and his gunner fired covering mine. It had the desired effect. The enemy gunners kept their heads down till we were almost out of range and then the few desultory shots were of little account.

'We arrived back at base, somewhat battered but still intact with all five aircraft coming into the circuit together. After debriefing, I sat in a chair with a cup of coffee and a cigarette, utterly relaxed. This is one of the things about operational flying that I remember most vividly. The feeling of relaxation, so complete that I felt I could sit there for ever.'

Low-Level Casualty

Flt Lt Aubrey Niner

'I flew Douglas Bostons with No 88 Squadron RAF from October 1941, until a fateful low-level mission on 19 July 1942, when I was shot down. The operational order called for No 88 Squadron and No 226 Squadron of 2 Group Bomber Command, to bomb from low level the Lomme, France, power station. This target was located near the city of Lille. Aircraft were to fly in formation in pairs. Take-off time was 1400 hours. No 226 Squadron was to bomb the same target but approach from a different direction five minutes after No 88 Squadron.

'We took off at about 1400 hours – my crew consisting of Philip Jacobs, observer and George Lawman, gunner and radio operator.

I was leading G. (Ginger) Attenborough, pilot and "Tubby" Murdock, observer, who were flying on my port side. The trip was uneventful under low 10/10th cloud and Philip Jacobs navigated us on track.

'A few minutes short of the target it was necessary to turn fairly sharply to port and at that moment we went into low cloud. (It is possible that because we were flying low I instinctively gained a little height to make room for the No 2 aircraft who in the turn was on my port side and, therefore, below me.)

'When we came out of cloud, I found that we were off to the right of the target whereas Ginger Attenborough who probably tightened his turn in the cloud was heading directly for it.

'He dropped his bombs and I decided that in view of the ideal conditions for low-level flying he was safe to go home alone and we were safe to go around again. I told Ginger to "go home".

'After we were clear of Lille and flying very low, Philip Jacobs gave me a course to fly to bring us back over the target. I then turned

Below: Flt Lt Aubrey Niner's Boston III after he had successfully crash landed it near Lille, France. / Niner

to starboard and immediately saw tracer coming at us almost horizontally from the pivot of my turn.

'George Lawman then reported flames from the port engine and it immediately cut out. I feathered the propeller and tried the extinguisher but the flames continued. We were than at low level, on one engine with bombs on and bomb doors open. As we approached the target area we crossed an airfield and with Philip Jacobs bomb aiming we dropped our bombs on the control tower.

'The next moment we were flying through the smoke and explosions of the attack by No 226 Squadron. I saw that the flames from the engine were buckling the plates on the wing and George Lawman reported that he was getting "bloody hot".

'Although my technical knowledge of the principles of aircraft construction were nil, I did know that the Boston was of stressed skin construction and it seemed to me that if the fire continued for long the skin of the wing would be damaged to the point where the wing would break off. I therefore was determined to land and I then saw trees and a patch of green among the buildings straight ahead. I put on full flap and landed with gear retracted.

'We all emerged safely although Philip Jacobs had bruised his leg on the bombsight. We were taken to Luftwaffe HQ in Lille and then by train to Brussels where we spent the first night in the Brussels jail. The next day we went by train to Frankfurt and spent three weeks in Dulag Luft at Obauresel. I then went to Stalag Luft III and Philip and George went to a camp at Larnsdorf.'

Intruder Pilot

Plt Off Arthur Bird

'I joined No 23 Squadron RAF, at Ford in Sussex when they were still flying their early intruder operations in Bristol Blenheims. In January 1941 I flew my first Havoc Mark I. This aircraft had been originally made for the French and all instrumentation was in metres and kilometres, but that didn't detract from the fact that it was a tremendous aircraft to fly.

'The Havoc did give us a few difficulties in the beginning. None of us were accustomed to the handling of an aircraft with tricycle landing gear and this took some getting used to. The single disc hydraulic brakes caused a number of slipping and skidding accidents until we reduced the hydraulic pressure in the system for operations on grass fields.

'From a pilot's standpoint the aircraft was excellent. It was a very stable machine to fly and I have always felt that the dihedral in the tail had a lot to do with this. The cockpit was comfortable and roomy and all controls were easily accessible. Visibility from the cockpit was excellent.

'Night intruder flying in the Havoc gave us no particular problems. Our assignment was to seek and destroy enemy aircraft over their own bases on the Continent. Due to the fact that we were carrying a 1,000lb bomb load on these missions in addition to our intruder duties our range was limited. Our operations took us over a regular route of airfields in France, Belgium and Holland. We navigated by dead reckoning and we did have a bit of trouble initially with the compasses in the Havocs. The difficulty was traced to the fact that the front oleo leg of the landing gear was magnetised which was taking us far off course. Demagnetising of the gear corrected this defect.

'No 23 Squadron normally sent out three aircraft each night, with A and B Flights alternating. On the evening of 13 August 1941, I reported to operations along with two other crews for the events of the evening. The weather was doubtful and it was decided that in view of the fact that I had the only experienced crew that I would go out alone. Intelligence reported that some 30 Heinkel He111s were returning from mine laying operations in the Thames Estuary plus other reports of Junkers Ju88s practising night landings at their airfields in France. It gave indications of an interesting evening and it was.

'I took-off along with my observer, Sgt Morris, and air gunner Sgt Campbell, from Manston at 0040 hours en route to patrol Gilze-Rijen airfield in Holland. We crossed the Belgian coast at Nieuport at an altitude of 8,500ft and proceeded to the target area. Our Havoc was over the target area at 0133 hours and I dropped through scattered cloud cover and found a clearing through which a beacon was flashing YV or VY.

'While still flying at 5,000ft I sighted a red cartridge fired from the direction of the airfield. As I continued to circle and lose height, the airfield lights and flarepath came on together with the long line of visual border landing lights. As we dropped down to 3,000ft one enemy aircraft was seen to land, using his landing lights. After landing, he turned left and taxied toward a dispersal area on the east side of the airfield. At this time we sighted three to five enemy aircraft with navigation lights on flying round the circuit at 2,000-3,000ft. Now and again their navigation lights would be switched off. These enemy aircraft occasionally flashed their landing lights while they were flying at 1,000ft along the long line of lights leading to the airfield. The latter was clearly indicated by its red boundary lights. These leading-in lights were approximately five miles long; at least six times the diameter of the airfield.

'I fired at the first enemy aircraft as he was approaching the runway at approximately 500ft. The attack was made with the four front .30 calibre guns from 25 degrees to port beam. No results were observed with the first burst, but bullets were seen striking after the second burst, which was made at 50yd range. The enemy aircraft's lights were switched off. I claimed this as a "damaged".

'At the same time that I was attacking the first enemy aircraft, Sgt Campbell fired the top rear gun at another enemy aircraft. He saw his bullets hitting and this aircraft was also claimed as "damaged". As we broke away and climbed the airfield lights were

Right: Plt Off Arthur 'Dickie' Bird (centre) and his crew; Sgt Morris (left) and Sgt Campbell (right).
/ Bird

Below: *Dickie's Clipper* The Havoc Mk I flown by Plt Off Arthur Bird in No 23 Squadron RAF in 1941.
/ Bird

switched off and we flew into the clouds to hide a bit.

'Shortly afterwards, I broke out of the clouds and found my self on the east side of the airfield, which was again lit up, and one enemy aircraft was making an approach along the leading-in lights, while another enemy aircraft was very low down over the extreme North-West corner of the airfield. A five star red cartridge was fired from this aircraft.

'Sgt Campbell then fired at a third enemy aircraft which was coming towards us, across our course, and this aircraft passed beneath us going down with his navigation lights still on. We claimed this aircraft "damaged".

'I fired on the fourth enemy aircraft from above and from our port beam with my front guns. Bullets were seen to strike this aircraft which I claimed as "damaged".

'As I manoeuvred into position for another attack Sgt Campbell loosed a burst at still another enemy aircraft off our port side, but no hits were observed.

'I sighted another enemy bomber below and to the left and I nosed down on him opening fire with my nose guns. I gave him a long burst and held it until I was buffeted by his slipstream. When last seen this aircraft turned over and away from its original course of landing and continued to go down in the opposite direction. It is considered unlikely that this aircraft could pull out of a dive at such a low altitude and I claimed a "probable".

'As I broke off my attack Sgt Campbell asked me to raise the nose of the Havoc to enable him to get at another enemy aircraft. Two long bursts were put into this bomber which was astern and at approximately 500ft coming in to land. Campbell saw the flashes of his bullets striking the front of the aircraft at which time it broke sharply to the right and nosed down steeply with its navigation lights still on. I feel that this aircraft also didn't make it to the airfield and so claimed a "probable" for Sgt Campbell.

'For a final gesture we made another pass across the dispersal area and dropped our bombs; 18 x 40lb GP and 60 x 4lb incendiaries. Sgt Campbell saw the bombs burst amongst the huts and buildings, one of which caused a vivid green flash.

'I then set course and headed home.'

First of the Many A-20s over Europe

The 15th Bombardment Squadron (Light) was originally formed in April 1942 as the First Pursuit Squadron to be trained as night fighters to reinforce Royal Air Force units in the United Kingdom.

Following their training at Lawson Field just outside Fort Benning, Georgia the unit left the United States on 1 May 1942, for England. Upon arrival they were informed that the Royal Air Force was no longer in need of further night fighter squadrons and that First Pursuit were to become a light bombardment squadron flying Douglas Bostons borrowed from the British.

The Americans were attached to No 226 Squadron RAF for training and by the end of June 1942 were proficient in their duties. On the afternoon of 29 June 1942, Capt Charles C. Kegelman along with his bombardier, Lt Bell, and gunners, Sgts Golay and Cunningham, joined a formation of 12 Bostons under the command of Sqn Ldr Kennedy on a 'circus' to Hazebrouck marshalling yards. This crew became the first of the US Army Air Forces to bomb territory in enemy-occupied Europe.

Following this mission it was decided that the Americans should carry out their first operational strike in numbers on American Independence Day, 4 July. On that day six American crews headed by Capt Charles C. Kegelman, William C. Odell, Martin P. Crabtree and Lts Leo Hawel, Frederick A. Loehrl and William G. Lynn, Jr joined six Royal Air Force crews from No 226 Squadron under the command of Sqn Ldr J. S. Kennedy bound for enemy airfields in Holland.

The Bostons formed up and headed across the Channel at low level. Unfortunately, they flew right over two of the German 'squealer' boats which were used to inform the enemy that a mission was en route.

Enemy flak came up immediately the Bostons crossed the Dutch coast. The trio composed of Sqn Ldr Kennedy, Capt Kegelman and Lt Loehrl pressed on through intense fire to get at the airfield at De Kooy. All pilots had been emphatically instructed to make all approaches and runs flat and very low. There were to be no steep turns, even off the target. To accomplish this Kennedy

nearly crashed. He was so low that in one of his flat turns one wing scraped the ground. Lt Loehrl didn't remember to keep his turns flat. A steep banking turn presented the Boston to the flak gunners in full silhouette. The aircraft took a direct hit which blew the nose off. The aircraft burst into flames and crashed into shallow water near the airfield.

Capt Kegelman kept so low that one of his propellers struck the ground, wrenching it completely off. Hugging the ground Kegelman made good his escape from the flak area and managed to get his badly damaged aircraft to the dubious safety of the North Sea.

The second trio of Bostons swept over the airfield at Bergen. There they dropped their bombs amidst intense, heavy flak. One gun position succeeded in putting shots into Lt William G. Lynn's Boston and his aircraft crashed a few miles north of the airfield. A second Boston from this trio fell to the guns of a Messerschmitt Bf109. Plt Off Henning of the RAF went down at sea west of Den Helder.

The other six Bostons struck the airfields at Hamstede and Valkenburg. The attack on Hamstede scored some good hits, but the leader of the trio that attacked Valkenburg failed to open his doors soon enough for bombing, so all the airfield suffered was a brief strafing.

Eight of the Bostons returned to base at Swanton Morley in good order, but upon their landing and debriefing there was still no sight of Capt Kegelman. The surviving Americans were huddled around a then 'unknown' American officer by the name of Eisenhower who had come to see them in. As they related their stories of the mission a lone Boston was sighted limping in to the airfield. Kegelman had managed to come home with his Boston.

Above: Capt Charles Kegelman. He led the first USAAF detachment that accompanied No 226 Squadron RAF on the Americans' first mission over Europe on 4 July 1942. / USAF

D-Day: The 409th Bomb Group

F. Morrow

'I was aroused from my sleep at 0300 hours on the morning of 6 June 1944. I pulled on my clothes and went up the hill for briefing. As we assembled the men anxiously awaited the arrival of the Intelligence Officer who would remove the sheet that covered the map on the wall that would show our target for the day.

'Upon his arrival he began briefing with, "Men, this is the day you have been waiting for. The invasion of France has begun." He then proceeded to fill us in on the details of D-Day and then briefed us on our target for the day which was a strategic road junction near Bologne. It was imperative that this junction be destroyed to prevent the movement of panzer units to the beachhead.

Left: The effectiveness of the A-20 is exemplified by the pitted runway of this enemy airfield. The A-20 did tremendous work in knocking out airfields throughout their campaign in the ETO. / *USAF*

Below: Donald F. Morrow and *Skip*, the A-20 on which he flew his memorable D-Day mission. / *Morrow*

'Following briefing we donned our flying clothes and loaded on the 6 x 6 trucks that dropped us off at our respective aircraft. As engineer gunner it was my duty to check the aircraft to see that it had been properly serviced and that everything was operationally serviceable.

'Once the aircraft had been checked out there was nothing to do but wait for the tower to fire the green flare that indicated that the mission was on and it was time to start the engines. We didn't have long to wait and Sgt Duncan and I climbed in the rear and Lt Murphy cranked up the engines.

'We taxied out to the end of the runway and the A-20s began to take-off into the murky sky at 15-second intervals. Once airborne the squadron assembled quickly and in a very short while we were flying out over the Channel. The waters below were literally covered with every kind of naval vessel imaginable. We made landfall and headed directly for the target. Soon our squadron bombardier picked up the target and we went in amid moderate flak and dropped our four 500lb bombs. Lt Murphy then began a zig-zag course for home. We sighted a few enemy fighters in the area but none of them made any attempt to intercept. In no time at all we were back at home base.

'As soon as we taxied in and parked our ground crews began readying the aircraft for another mission. This time we were to go 40 miles inland to hit a marshalling yard where panzer troops were reported assembling.

'We took off and assembled – a force of 28 A-20s flying at 12,000ft. As we neared the coast we encountered solid 10/10ths cloud cover below us. The aircraft began to break formation and we made individual penetration of the cloud cover. We broke out right on the deck and assembled with six other A-20s. As we roared over the French countryside our pilot told us to strafe any ground targets we sighted. I got down and manned my .50 calibre gun in the lower tunnel but the "tail-end Charlie" aircraft in our formation had his nose tucked in so tight that I couldn't fire for fear of hitting him. Finally he dropped back and I was able to use my gun.

Above: An A-20J of the
646th Bombardment Squadron,
410th Bombardment Group. The
bombardier used his sight over the
target and the gun-nosed aircraft
salvoed their bombs when he
released his. / *USAF*

Left: An outward bound A-20
newly marked with invasion stripes
and bomb laden to strike at enemy
targets in France. / *USAF*

'Once the target was sighted the A-20s pulled up until they were just scraping the clouds in an attempt to gain altitude. It was not recommended to drop 500lb bombs with instantaneous fuses from under 1,000ft.

'All of a sudden I felt a blast of cold air from up forward and Duncan told me that flak had shot out half of the plexiglass from his turret. I bent back over my gun to continue my strafing of ground targets and another blast hit the A-20 and I felt something strike my back. Some pieces of flak had ripped through the tunnel and fragments had hit my flak jacket and one piece ripped a hole in the toe of Duncan's flying boot.

'As we swept down on the target our left engine took a hit which severed an oil line. As oil sprayed over the engine, Lt Murphy immediately feathered the prop and dropped the bombs. Murphy ordered us to throw out all excess weight in order to maintain altitude. We threw out guns, ammunition and everything else we could find.

'As we roared out over the Channel, Lt Murphy pulled what altitude he could get so that when he turned on the IFF set air sea rescue could get a fix on us in case we had to ditch in the Channel. Just as we sighted the white cliffs there was a sudden silence. Our lone engine had quit. Immediately I made ready to bale out. Just as I started out the hatch the engine started up again. In his quest to find an emergency field for us to come in on Lt Murphy had neglected his fuel gauges and the engine had run out of fuel.

'Lt Murphy finally located the P-47 base at Saffron Walden and entered their pattern. Due to the fact that we had an engine out we were forced to fly the pattern backwards so as not to bank into the dead engine. We managed to come in OK, but the engine stopped right in the middle of the runway and there we sat. At this moment we looked down the runway and saw two P-47s bearing down on us. The first Thunderbolt hit his brakes to keep from running into us and he immediately nosed over. The second P-47 veered off the runway and went through a chestnut grove before he came to a stop. Needless to say, the CO of the P-47 outfit was very upset at losing two of his aircraft because we were sitting in the middle of his runway.

'When we surveyed our A-20 later that day we found that one flak hit had cut the right wing spar which necessitated the change of the wing. We counted 56 holes all told in the aircraft. In view of the fact that this aircraft had no name we decided that once repaired it should be called "Patches" and so it was.'

Below: A close-up view of the A-20G. This aircraft belonged to the 641st Bomb Squadron of the 409th Bomb Group. The 'G' carried six .50 calibre machine guns in the nose and had two .50 calibre guns in the power-driven Martin upper turret. / USAF

D-Day: No 342 Squadron

Paul Lambermont

'We practised dropping dummy bombs on to the Isle of Wight during combined exercises with commandos. And we laid smokescreens along the edge of woods, at treetop height.

'For this task the Boston's normal load of four 500lb bombs was replaced by smoke-containers – cylinders about eight feet long with exhaust pipes hanging down. The smoke escaping from four openings made up the screen.

'At last June came. Operations were virtually at a standstill. There was nothing to do. Hartford Bridge, our airfield was, in fact, at action stations.

'On 5 June, in the afternoon, I went to the dispersal point. I got my first hint. The mechanics were painting white bands on the wings and on the body of each Boston.

' "Yes," said my mechanic, "same treatment for all the Bostons and the Mitchells on the station. Make them into fine targets for the Huns' flak. We've also been ordered to keep all aircraft in readiness with smoke-containers aboard."

'I jumped on my bike and made record time to the officers' mess. Battle orders were posted. There were two of them: one for No 88 and one for my squadron, No 342.

'Twelve crews in each squadron were to stand by. On the No 342 list I read: Aircraft Q – Pilot Plt Off Clement, Navigator, Flg Off Lambermont, W/O P. Dorain.

'Briefing was at midnight. After a very early hurried breakfast, served by WAAFs half asleep, the standby crews made for the navigation room. Two maps with different itineraries were pinned to the rear wall. Threads of red wool stopped close to the French coast.

'At 0100 hours there was not a sound to be heard. Then the officer who had come specially from 2nd TAF HQ explained the part the Bostons were to play in the landings.

Below: Ordnance men of No 342 'Lorraine' Squadron get bombs ready to be loaded aboard their Bostons. Note the greeting to Hitler on one of the projectiles.
/ *Lambermont*

' "As I'm speaking to you now, the Royal Navy and the US Navy are already on their way to the Continent. Some of the vessels will already be at their destination before daybreak. *Warspite*, *Rodney* and other ships will be between the mouth of the Orne and the northern part of Bayeaux.

' "To hide them from fire from German coastal batteries, No 88 Squadron will lay a smokescreen between the vessels and the famous Atlantic Wall. To make the screen longer, aircraft will operate in pairs, following each other at ten minute intervals.

' "No 342 will be responsible for laying a screen in front of the American invasion fleet off the Cotentin peninsula, between St Marcouf Island and Barfleur Point."

'Then came practical advice. "To be effective the screen must start at the level of the waves. As the wind is blowing from south-west you won't have any trouble. When you lay the screen turn your oxygen on full. It's unwise to breathe in any of the smoke that might get forced back into the aircraft."

'I carefully noted the route in my log and checked over my navigation figures. The operations was expected to last 95min. At 0300 hours I was completely ready. I went back to my Nissen hut, going over the points in the briefing. I didn't sleep a wink.

'At 0545 hours I got into my parachute kit, more slowly then usual. I checked my Mae West, tested my mike, made sure that the oxygen to my mask worked properly. Sitting on my dinghy and with my safety belt fastened, I spread my charts and log. The two 1,800hp engines were already running. The mechanic lifted his thumbs into the air. Our Boston reached the entrance to the runway. Then at full power we took-off and the tricycle landing gear disappeared from view.

'Over still sleeping towns and villages we flew at more then 230mph. In 20min we reached the sea. As far as the eye could see there were craft of every kind – an incredible criss-cross of funnels, masts and tiny balloons kissing the clouds.

'Suddenly we saw France, right ahead, standing out of the water. The land came quickly at us. We were only 20ft above the waves. As we turned every gun in every battery on the Atlantic Wall was firing all out The American vessels facing them followed suit. Visibility – roughly eight miles – was better than our briefing had led us to expect.

'In a few minutes we'd have to get in between the two opposing sides. I adjusted my oxygen mask. On the intercom I heard: "Everyone OK? Oxygen on full."

'Without warning huge columns of water shot up in front of us. The Boston shook to its last rivet. A shell aimed short – by the Germans or the Allies we knew not – had landed a few yards from our aircraft.

'The time had come. I pressed the bomb-release button and a miracle happened. An endless stream of thick white smoke belched out behind the Boston, now doing 260mph. For a few moments the screen, eight miles long, hid the American armada. When the four containers were empty I gave the pilot the route back and let out a long "phew" of contentment.

'At 0730 hours our Boston touched down at Hartford Bridge and by 0800 all the others should have been back. But there were some casualties.

'One No 342 aircraft had exploded close to an Allied cruiser – a huge sheet of flame rapidly extinguished by the sea water. Its navigator, Bernard Canut, had a few hours earlier got rid of all his personal belongings. He gave his books to one friend and his ring to another. With his mechanic he'd left a letter to his family. In it he'd written, "I know I shan't come back."

'Another Boston from No 88 Squadron safely laid its smokescreen ahead of the Royal Navy, but then crashed on returning to Hartford Bridge. In no time the runway was a holocaust. It was the last aircraft to land there that day.

'On the D-Day the sky was burdened with more than 6,000 aircraft. Of those a mere 24 formed the advance guard of the gigantic landing armada. Of the 24, 12 were flown by No 342 Squadron. I was proud to be with them.'

Below: A Boston IV gets ready to set down in France for the first time. No 342 Squadron moved to the Continent in autumn 1944.
/ Lambermont

Above: *Chattanooga Belle*, an A-20G of the 643rd Squadron, 416th Bomb Group seeks out its target over France in the summer of 1944. / *Col R. Brown*

D-Day:
The 416th Group

Thirty-six A-20s of the 416th Bombardment Group took off for France on a cloud-covered afternoon, flying their second mission of D-Day. The leader's radio went out, the second box and three aircraft from the first box got separated in the overcast . . . that left 14. Capt Richard K. Bills, the deputy leader, led them in at 4,000ft to bomb a German strongpoint that threatened the beachhead. They bombed the target, despite flak damage on the way in and came back, despite more flak and icing on the way out. This is the way he experienced it that day as related by Capt Richard Bills on his return from the mission.

'On 6 June – D-Day – we were scheduled for a mission in the late afternoon. In this case "we" means my crew, Lt Michael W. McEvilly, bombardier-navigator, S/Sgt William A. Meldrum, turret gunner, and S/Sgt Charles L. Hyroad, tunnel gunner and myself. We were sweating the mission out, as the weather was so poor that most of the birds were walking.

'Finally the teletype order for the mission came into the situation room where the leaders wait for their pre-briefing. We were scheduled to fly deputy leader of the first box of 18 aircraft. When we got the complete set-up. we found that the target was of vital importance and that we were to bomb at 12,000ft, but if the ceiling were low, we were to drop as low as 2,000ft. The most dangerous altitude for a plane like ours in combat in the ETO was 1,000-5,000ft. So we began to sweat some more. Of course, we knew that the guys on the beaches were having a rough time, so flak or no flak, weather or no weather, we had to give them that aerial support.

'We took-off at our proper interval, and the formation joined up, with us flying on the leader's right wing. As we made our first circle of the field, the leader gave me the signal to take over because his radio had gone out completely. We went into the lead, and were instructed from the control tower to lead our box, but to follow the second box in. By this time the weather was so poor that we couldn't see the second box, which had set out on course, so we set our course and tried to catch up to them.

'On the way to the Channel, we endeavoured to get as high as we could, but each time we gained altitude, we lost it promptly due to an ever-lowering ceiling. We started across the Channel at about 3,000ft. Our hopes rose as we found we could gain about 5,000ft when we got to the middle of the Channel, but they fell with the altitude when we had to go under some more clouds.

'At this point, McEvilly noticed that there were only three ships in our number three flight, the other three apparently having turned back. This left only five aircraft in my flight and six in my number two flight, making a total of 14 in the box.

'In another few minutes, we hit some more very low clouds and our whole number two flight got separated from us, plus one more ship from the number three flight, leaving us only seven aircraft. We reached the French coast at 4,000ft, circled once to see if our other planes could find us and also to make sure that we were at the right place of entry, as visibility was less than a mile. Then we went in.

'The instant we got within range of the guns, they started shooting. We were getting light and heavy flak in intense and accurate doses. The only evasive action we could take was a constant weaving which at least made the ground gunners move their guns, if nothing else. McEvilly was talking to me all the time, pointing out the landmarks, so I'd know we were on course. The two gunners were pretty calm and cool, considering the amount of flak being sent up. Every few seconds I'd look the plane over, along with those of my wing men, and even at this point, I could see quite a few holes in fuselages and wings. Everyone was still in tight formation, however, and seemed to be running OK. The gunners were coming through with classic remarks such as Meldrum's "Hey, Skipper, I think someone out there doesn't like us."

'Suddenly McEvilly called out, "Here's our IP" (Initial Point for the bomb run.) At the same instant, I saw what I thought was our first box ahead of us, and also the target. At this point I was quite excited, as our navigation was working out perfectly despite poor visibility. The A-20s in front of us were catching hell and it was as bad to watch them as it was to be in it ourselves. They had already settled down on their target run when the proverbial hell broke loose. A box barrage of 1,500-2,000 bursts of heavy flak came up just as they dropped their bombs and three ships burst into flames from direct hits. We couldn't watch them any longer, as we were near enough to begin our target run, and we had to settle down to straight and level flying.

'We were pretty silent now, as we had all seen what happened ahead of us, and were tightening ourselves up, expecting the worst. McEvilly was busy on his sight and I took a quick look around. All aircraft were still there and flying OK, but my own aircraft had a lot of holes in it. Even as I watched, I saw two four-inch holes appear in the left wing as if by magic. Mike was saying "Steady – left – left – ", and then the long awaited, "Bombs away".

'With bombs gone, I made a steep diving turn left and had a chance to look around again. What I saw didn't please me. There were at least 2,000 bursts of heavy flak filling the sky around us and light flak tracers were coming from every direction. I had decided to hit for the deck and come out fast, but as we were diving down, the flak increased and McEvilly hollered over the intercom, "I don't think we'll ever get down in one piece."

'After taking a quick look around I decided he was right. Looking ahead I saw a low-lying bank of clouds so we headed for them, still weaving and bobbing like a broken field runner. We were at about 2,500ft and Meldrum was shooting at the flak positions. It helped keep his morale up, and he swears he killed "hundreds of them".

'It was about at this point that I felt my rudder pedals swing free and informed the boys that my rudder pedals were out. The A-20 was flying pretty well though and we were just going into the cloud bank when Hyroad told me that one of our planes appeared to be going down or at least had dropped out of formation.

'An important point I forgot to mention is that we got a good look at the target as we turned away and we had hit it squarely. At this time, however, we were too busy to be elated over that.

'The cloud cover was working swell, as it was thick enough to screen us but thin enough for us to keep our formation. Suddenly, however, we ran smack through some heavy clouds and got separated from all but one A-20. As I checked my aircraft over I noticed the oil pressure was dropping and at the same time my fuel pressure was low. This spelled single engine operation to me, which on instruments is rather difficult, and with no rudder is next to impossible. I checked my trim tab and found it OK. I warned McEvilly and the gunners to be ready to jump at an instant's notice. If the trim tab didn't compensate for the rudder I'd have to cut the good engine and abandon ship.

'As if we didn't have enough trouble, we started getting ice. In less than a minute, we had an inch of it on the wings and the ship was feeling heavy. But by this time I decided the engine would be OK for if it were going to stop it should have stopped already.

'All this time, Lt Thomas Kirkpatrick in the lone A-20 with us had stuck to us somehow. He was just sort of a blur most of the time and sometimes we couldn't see him at all. But he hung on with the tenacity of a bulldog, and surely had our admiration for the flying he was doing.

'Now we were emerging from the clouds and could see water ahead, but we were still over land. We had about 90sec to fly for the coast and they started shooting again. We were all mad by now so we flew right out in the open but did take the precaution of a little weaving. With a parting flurry of heavy and light flak the enemy bade us farewell for the afternoon.

'Out over the Channel we took stock. No one was hit, although a piece of flak broke the glass in the nose were Mike had bent over his sight. Our A-20 was a sieve, but still flying with both engines still running. The left engine sounded rough, and as all the engine instruments were shot out I couldn't tell much about it.

'As we neared the English coast, we had a conference to determine whether to make for the base or land at an emergency field and chose the latter as the most sensible answer. I tried to contact Kirkpatrick, but had no luck, so I waved him on. He left us and headed for base. I tried to contact some field but my radio was out. Luck was with us in having the intercom working so we could talk to each other. Mike gave me the course to the nearest field and we went in to land.

'After making a wide circle of the field we came in on the approach. I didn't want to make any steep turns without a rudder so it took us four minutes to circle the field. As we settled down onto the field, we could see people watching. It was an emergency field and they figured something was likely to happen. There was a strong cross wind and I knew we would hit crooked as the plane couldn't be straightened up at the last instant. Suddenly we hit and started to bump along. I knew without looking that we had a flat tyre and warned the boys to hold on. We were moving left towards a steep embankment, but we stopped right on the edge of it. I breathed a sigh of relief, got out and wanted to kiss the ground.

Below: The A-20s of the 416th Bomb Group in bright new invasion stripes set out to hit German strongpoints on D-Day. / USAF

'We had two flat tires, which accounted for the rough landing. The A-20 was really a sieve, and the holes ranged from four inch gaps to what looked like bullet holes. The gunner's compartment was covered with flak holes. The rudder cables were cut and all the engine instruments on the left engine had been shot out. Two of our gas tanks had holes. The plane was a mess but hadn't been hit in a vital spot.

'We agreed that we were over the hump. If Jerry couldn't get us that day, he had wasted his best chance.'

Bostons in North Africa and Italy

The Boston III saw its initial action with No 24 Squadron of the South African Air Force stationed in the Western Desert. This unit got a limited number of the aircraft and began using them for reconnaissance work as early as November 1941. The aircraft usually went out alone and had to prove their ability to deal with enemy fighters the hard way and, unfortunately, several Bostons fell victim to Bf109s and Bf110s on this type of operation.

By 5 December 1941, No 24 Squadron had 10 Bostons operational and was assigned to No 3 South African Wing flying from Landing Ground No 130. Tragically 10 December brought about an unfortunate mission on which the Boston bomber suffered its heaviest losses of any one operation in North Africa. Once more, the Bostons of No 24 Squadron were sent out unescorted. Six Bostons under the command of Maj E. N. Donnelly were dispatched to attack retreating German troops in the vicinity of Laib Esem.

As they approached the target they had the misfortune of encountering a formation of Messerschmitt Bf109s which were escorting Stuka dive bombers. The 109s immediately initiated an attack on the Bostons. Lt Jim Williams, No 3 man in the rear flight was the first to be hit. An attack from the rear had severely wounded the gunners and set the aircraft on fire. Williams gave the bale out order, but before the men could get out the aircraft was hit in the tail section once more. Williams rose to abandon ship and noted that one of his wounded gunners was still not out. He sat back and struggled with the controls to keep the aircraft level until the gunner got out. When Williams himself left he was down to 1,500ft.

Next to be hit was the Boston flown by Lt G. Genis. It was set on fire and Genis headed for a cloud layer to give the crew time to bale out. Only the observer managed to get out, the rest of the crew being too badly wounded to leave the aircraft. The Boston flown by Capt F. W. Goch was also set on fire and although Goch and his observer managed to get out Goch later died from wounds and injuries.

The third Boston of the leading flight was also shot down with a wing in flames. The pilot and two gunners managed to get out just before the wing fell off.

Below: Despite heavy losses in their early operations, the men of Nos 12 and 24 Squadrons SAAF came to appreciate their Bostons when fighter escort kept the Bf 109s at bay. / IWM

Top: Desert sand gave the South African squadrons much initial difficulty. New engines often didn't last a dozen hours. A new air filter rectified this problem. / IWM

Above: No 12 Squadron SAAF sets out to hit one of the North African targets. The Bostons did fine work in North Africa against airfields and harbour installations. / IWM

Left: South African Boston IIIs in echelon. Their gunners had to perfect coverage of each other in formation to have any hope of driving off Luftwaffe fighters. / IWM

Left: A-20Bs of the 47th Bombardment Group over North Africa. Note the yellow circle around the blue national insignia. / USAF

Below: A-20s of the 47th Bomb Group in formation over the Mediterranean. The 47th was the only A-20 bomb group in the theatre representing the USAAF, but they did a tremendous job of tactical air support. / USAF

Right: Weathered and battered A-20B of the 47th Bomb Group over the desolation that was North Africa. Note the single .50 calibre installation in the rear. / USAF

Below right: One of two RAF squadrons to receive the Boston III in the Mediterranean was No 114 Squadron. One of their aircraft is shown here in May 1943. Note dispersal area in the upper right hand corner. / C. Bowyer

Only one Boston managed to escape; that of Maj Donnelly. He managed to crash land his severely damaged aircraft near Landing Ground 76. This disastrous mission became known tc No 24 Squadron as 'The Boston Tea Party'.

Only a few more operations were flown by No 24 Squadron before they were withdrawn from combat on 23 December. However losses were not the primary reason for the withdrawal. The engines of the Bostons were suffering from excessive oil consumption and some were having to be changed with as few as 10 hours' flying time. All the engines had to be modified and fitted with a new type of air filter which solved the problem.

By 22 February 1942, the Bostons of No 24 Squadron were back in action at full strength. From this time on, however, the bombers were not sent out without escort for the German fighters in North Africa became daily more numerous and aggressive as was illustrated a few days after the squadron returned to action. A formation of three Bostons were taking-off from Baherira bound for El Daba when they were attacked by two Bf109s. The Boston flown by Lt T. J. P. Botha burst into flames and only an extraordinary effort by the pilot brought the plane in on its belly. The crew escaped but flames prevented them from saving their gallant pilot.

By March 1942 the forces in North Africa received another welcome reinforcement when

No 12 Squadron of the South African Air Force began operations in Bostons. Like No 24 Squadron, they, too, had flown the Martin Maryland before getting the new attack bombers. Both squadrons teamed up on 15 March for a successful mission against Martuba West Landing Ground. Eight Bostons from No 24 Squadron and four from No 12 Squadron scored direct hits on five enemy aircraft and they damaged another eight.

The Bostons of both squadrons saw considerable action during Rommel's retreat at the end of May. They flew a number of missions against the German motor columns and destroyed many enemy troops and vehicles. At last light on 29 May Bostons of No 24 Squadron attacked an enemy shipping convoy at Derna. In spite of very heavy flak the Bostons went in at 1,000ft and got good strikes on ships in the harbour. One Boston and its crew were lost on the mission.

Throughout the summer of 1942 the two squadrons of Bostons continued to hit at German airfields, motor columns and troop concentrations. As reinforcements arrived both squadrons were brought up to full strength. With sufficient escort and battle experience behind them the Boston crews struck out at the enemy from dawn until late at night.

The climax in North Africa came on the night of 23 October 1942, when the great El Alamein offensive began. The two Boston squadrons were assigned to lay smokescreens in advance of the ground troops. To accomplish this at night at an altitude of 30-50ft took considerable practice on the part of the crews. Shortly after midnight Capt J. P. de Villiers of No 12 Squadron laid down a two mile smokescreen between the enemy and the 9th Australian Division. Helped by flares from the ground, they continued their smoke laying operation until dawn despite heavy small arms fire and continuous minor damage.

At first light the Bostons continued their raids hitting enemy targets. Very heavy fire was encountered from the panzer and

armoured columns and the Bostons suffered heavy casualties. The official daily operational summary stated, 'Five Bostons shot down ... seven badly shot up ... not a single aircraft without at least ten holes.'

The first Bostons of the USAAF entered combat in North Africa following the Allied invasion on 2 November 1942. The 15th Bombardment Squadron which had flown the first European mission of the USAAF from England had been tabbed to go to North Africa in September 1942. This unit left Predannack on the south coast of England flying non-stop to La Seina airport at Oran on 8 November 1942. The next day they moved to Maison Blanc airport at Algiers. Two days later the 15th moved to the mountains at Youk Les Bains, where they operated from a mud field named Tebessa. From mid-November through mid-January 1943, the 15th flew two and often three missions a day against Bizerte, Gabes and Gafsa.

They were relieved by the 47th Bombardment Group which came to North Africa directly from the United States. (The 47th would do yeoman duty in the Mediterranean theatre for the rest of the war.) It initially distinguished itself when German forces broke through at Kasserine Pass in February 1943. The A-20s of the 47th flew 11 missions on 22 February to attack the German panzer forces and help stop the enemy's offensive and for this action the 47th was awarded its first Distinguished Unit Citation.

As British forces attacked from the east and American forces from the west, the German Afrika Korps was pushed into Tunisia and finally defeated. Boston operations from both sides destroyed a myriad of aircraft and motor transport and did much to help bring about the final victory in North Africa.

Next targets for the Bostons were on the island of Pantelleria whose garrison fell to airpower in June 1943. Then came the island

Below: *Tutu*, a gunship of the 47th Bomb Group. The plexiglass nose has been painted over and .50 calibre machine guns installed for strafing. Note the mission stars below the pilot's window. / *USAF*

56

of Sicily and once more the Bostons were there striking at enemy airfields and troop concentrations. Typical of the pre-invasion strikes were those of the 47th Group.

'On 1 July 12 A-20s struck at Sciacca Airdrome. A bomb pattern 500ft long and 200ft wide was laid across the south portion of the landing ground. One large fire was started and one large explosion was seen to result from the bombing. Intense, heavy, accurate flak was encountered . . .

'On 9 July two enemy fighters were shot down and credit for these given to Capt Tourtellet and S/Sgt Krause. The target was again Sciacca Aerodrome. Smoke and fires were seen in the bombed area. Intense, heavy and accurate flak was encountered in the entire target area. Four Bf109s and three Fw190s attacked the formation on the breakaway after the bomb run. S/Sgt Krause fired his guns at an attacking ship and the Fw190 was seen to go down in smoke and flame. A Bf109 which attacked the lead box was hit by Capt Tourtellet's .50 calibre gun and seen to drop in a spin. Other enemy planes sighted, which did not attack, were three Reggiane Re2001s and two Macchi C200s. Three A-20s received major damage, while two received minor damage. All planes returned to base.'

Following the invasion of Sicily it was decided the distance was too great for the A-20s to give proper support to the ground forces so the 47th was transferred to the island of Malta. There they remained until their move to Sicily in early August 1943.

Converting to operations in Bostons in April 1943 were Nos 18 and 114 Squadrons RAF. Both of these units began their Boston operations in North Africa and continued to operate the aircraft in Sicily and Italy up to the end of the war.

No 12 and No 24 Squadrons of the South African Air Force continued operations in Bostons up until the end of 1944 at which time they converted to Martin Marauders.

Following the invasion of Italy and the Battle of Cassino in Italy the Bostons failed to encounter further enemy aircraft interceptions but the degree of flak that they had to brave became more and more intense as the war continued. However, the men of the Bostons continued to lead the way in tactical air operations up until the end of the war in Italy in 1945.

Top left: The 47th operated from Sicily alongside Spitfires of the RAF. The oxen don't seem to be bothered by either. / IWM

Bottom left: *Miss Burma* was a veteran of many missions with the 47th Group. The bombs painted under the co-pilot's window seem to run all the way down the fuselage. / USAF

Below: *Lana* bore the name and portrait of motion picture star Lana Turner on its nose. From the number of bombs painted below it would seem that *Lana* was a star performer over Italy, too. / USAF

A-20s at Kasserine Pass

Maj Gen Frederick Terrell USAF (Ret)

'My 47th Bombardment Group picked up A-20Bs in September 1942 in Kansas City, Missouri, where they had been modified for overwater ferry. We arrived in North Africa in November 1942 with 57 aircraft having lost three A-20s en route via Goose Bay, Labrador, Greenland, Iceland, Scotland and England.

'By February 1943, we had been in combat two months. My four squadrons were evenly split between two airfields, Thelepte in Tunisia and at Youks-Les-Bains, Algeria. We received targets and fighter escort assignment in various ways, mostly through 12th Air Support Command which was at Tebessa alongside II Corps Headquarters, US Army under the command of Gen George Patton. Since fighter aircraft were on our airdromes, full mission planning and tactics were worked out at combat unit level. Given the mobility and disbursement of ground forces, we did little close air support. Our targets were well beyond the area of friendly forces westward to the coastline and southward as far as the true desert. We used low-level attack against enemy armoured units, troop bivouacs and communications. Our formations were basically in four aircraft flights of two elements or sections, in loose echelon much like fighter aircraft "trail" formation. We used medium altitude (10,000-12,000ft) against coastal concentrations, harbours and enemy airfields flying in multiple six aircraft boxes.

'By mid-February 1943 II Corps was getting the worst of it south of us, around Gafsa and Macnassey and by the 15th of the month, US Armoured was pushed back through Faid Pass just to the north-east of Thelepte. We could see dust from ground level and could see derelict tanks out east of the Pass during our return from missions. We could hear artillery to the south by day and see the flashes by night. We were hit at dawn and dusk by beautifully timed Messerschmitt Bf109 sweeps; bombing and strafing. They burned a few of our aircraft but no personnel were seriously hurt during those days.

'About 17 or 18 February 12th Air Support Command told us to evacuate Thelepte. Our trucks departed during the night and we took-off at dawn. While circling Thelepte to allow formation form-up, I thought I saw artillery bursts in the aerodrome area. Afterwards at Youks, other pilots thought they had seen the same thing. The following day we bombed German panzers within sight of our home base of the day before.

'By 21 February we were operating at reduced group strength at Youks-Les-Bains, several of our aircraft having been left at Thelepte due to their damaged condition. During the night I received a phone call from Gen P. L. Williams, CG of 12th Air Support Command, informing me that I was in command of all forces at Youks (I had been promoted to full colonel two weeks before). I was also told that I was on my own to do whatever fighting I could. 12th Air Support Command and II Corps Headquarters were evacuating Tebessa and severing communications with me. German columns were last seen approaching Kasserine Pass.

'Along with our group at Youks-Les-Bains were US Spitfires, two batteries of British anti-aircraft, two battalions of French Infantry in the hills and the French Lafayette Escadrille flying US P-40s. The troops of II Corps were in the mountains and hills east of us, mostly south of Kasserine Pass. The weather was thick overcast.

'At daylight we had low cloud but the visibility was fair. I took an A-20 and skimmed over a ridge of hills to the north-east and found an open valley 2-5 miles wide stretching toward Kasserine Pass, which was some 12 or 15 miles away. The valley had two arms; the one that I was in and another stretching to the north. I had not been low level in this valley before. I could now see what looked like German armoured vehicles on the road along the east rim of the pass. Visibility was good under low cloud. I returned to base and was informed that our servicing squadron had left Youks during the night. I asked the men if they could service and load the bombs ourselves and they said we could.

'Gene Fletcher, Group Operations Officer, took over service and supply and I took over group operations. We organised flights of four aircraft to go in low level to strafe and skip bomb targets of opportunity. Three hundred pound bombs were all we had. We had modified some A-20s ourselves, adding up to six .50 calibre machine guns in the nose which we used to best advantage. We allowed one flight in the battle area at a time to avoid traffic problems. Each in turn was debriefed in the hearing of the next pilots to go. This running narrative told us that the German panzers were progressing up both arms of the valley toward us, as well as to the north. Later in the day the concentration was much heavier to the north. In the 10 or more hours of daylight then available, we sent out 11 missions, close to 44 sorties. Three of these all volunteer crews were shot down, and several men were wounded. Regardless, they had inflicted serious damage on the enemy which began its retreat from Kasserine Pass that night.

'The battle was over. I doubt that we could have mounted 24 aircraft for operations the next day.

'After Kasserine Pass we were re-trained for medium altitude and never returned to low level. We also tried the RAF bombsight which came along with RAF navigator-bombardier instructors who flew with us well into the summer.

'We had a good day in mid-March, our first big operation with mixed RAF/US crews. Flying out of Thelepte we put in over 100 sorties against German fighter aerodromes around La Fouconarri, behind the Mareth Line. We received personal citations from our new Allied Headquarters for clearing the air of German fighter aircraft and helping Field Marshal Montgomery to break through the Mareth Line.

'During this period we also gained some RAF officer-gunners. These men took position at Group Lead's upper gun and directed turns for massed defence against enemy fighters. This tactic along with tight formation made us very unattractive to the Messerschmitt Bf109s and Focke Wulf Fw190s. Henceforth, they deserted us and gave all their attention to the B-25s and B-26s. We enjoyed being in the air with our larger brothers. They were so attractive.'

Below: The paint job on the A-20 seems to blend in with the terrain below. The 47th Group made a business of bridge busting and transport strikes in the rugged Italian hills. / *USAF*

Below: Bombs away! A line of 23lb parafrags drop on Japanese targets. These bombs were most destructive to aircraft, buildings and personnel. / USAF

Bostons in the South-West Pacific

Left: The A-20 profile that would become famous in the South-West Pacific and bring disaster to the Japanese — low level with guns blazing. / *USAF*

Below: The 'Pappy' Gunn innovation that brought about the day of the gunships. / *USAF*

Right: Armourers remove fairing to service the .50 calibre guns on a SW Pacific gunship. / *USAF*

Below right: Flight of four Bostons from No 22 Squadron RAAF over low scattered clouds near Port Moresby, New Guinea in late 1942. / *RAAF via Smith*

Initial operations employing the Douglas A-20 in the South-West Pacific took place on 31 August 1942, when the 89th Squadron of the 3rd Bombardment Group went into action against Lae airdrome in New Guinea. Led by pilots like Capt Don Hall and Christian Pietre, the low-level attackers brought a new kind of war to the Japanese. More often than not the marauding A-20s coordinated their missions with the B-25 squadrons of the 3rd Group and kept the enemy off balance.

Through the ingenius work of one Maj 'Pappy' Gunn, the A-20s had been extensively modified to become 'gunships'. Instead of a glass nose for a bombardier the aircraft were fitted with six x .50 calibre machine guns. Some of the aircraft carried an additional two .50 calibre guns mounted in the wings.

The men of the 89th usually went in before the B-25 Mitchells who bombed from a higher altitude. The A-20s blazed in on the deck and caught the enemy aircraft on the ground and the gun crews scurrying to their anti-aircraft positions. The concentrated fire power of the gunships literally shot the enemy's aircraft and gun positions to pieces. While their specialty was airfields, the A-20s also did yeoman duty against light shipping and as support for ground forces in New Guinea.

Another innovation perfected by the men of the A-20s was the use of parafrags. These light 23lb bombs were dropped trailing small parachutes which gave the attackers time to get away from the target area before the explosion took place. The parafrags were used to best effect against enemy aircraft and ground installations.

The next unit to take the A-20 into combat in the South-West Pacific was No 22 Squadron of the Royal Australian Air Force. Three Bostons of No 22 carried out an armed reconnaissance along the coast from Sanananda Point to the mouth of the Kumuai River. During the Papuan campaign the Bostons of the RAAF flew continual missions against Japanese ground targets in support of Australian infantrymen advancing on Buna.

Another primary duty of not only the men of No 22 Squadron RAAF, but also for the men of the USAAF 89th Squadron was that of intercepting the numerous barges that the Japanese sent down the coast of New Guinea to reinforce and supply their troops in the Buna area. At other times the Japanese made high speed runs into the Buna area carrying troops aboard destroyers. These, too, were attacked by the Bostons with good results.

The climax of the operations against shipping reinforcements in the Buna area took place in March 1943 in the Battle of the Bismarck Sea. The triumphant story of 89 Squadron's participation in this historic operation is related in these pages by their

**Above: Bostons of No 22
Squadron RAAF on Neomfoor
Island. The RAAF adopted the
USAAF gun nose.**
/ RAAF via F. Smith

**Right: No 22 Squadron RAAF
over Kiriwina Island in the
Trobriands in November 1943. The
squadron did a tremendous job of
neutralising the Japanese air force
during the Battle of the Bismarck
Sea.** */ RAAF*

Above: DB-7 Boston *Indoor Sport* with No 22 Squadron RAAF seen at Wards Strip, Port Moresby in early 1943. / *RAAF via F. Smith*

leader, Capt Glen Clark. No 22 Squadron RAAF, also carried out a very important role in the battle. On the morning of 2 March, six Bostons swept in at treetop level over Lae airdrome where they proceeded to bomb and strafe the enemy aircraft and installations. Their excellent work prevented the Japanese from mounting covering air defences for their task force in the Bismarck Sea while American aircraft were assembling to bomb.

When the big coordinated attack took place the next morning the Bostons of No 22 Squadron repeated their attack on Lae aerodrome and were successful in keeping it completely neutralised while American aircraft, along with Australian Beaufighters, wrought devastation on the Japanese task force. When a second mission was mounted to strike the cripple remnants of the force, six Australian Bostons, led by Sqn Ldr C. C. Learmonth, attacked and managed to score several bomb hits on the surviving shipping. Their attacks came under constant attack from Japanese Zeros, but the Bostons were able to drive them off by turning into their attacks with their nose guns blazing.

Operations on 16 March 1943, set the stage for the gallant and tragic action which was to win for Flt Lt W. E. Newton the posthumous award of Britain's highest honour, the Victoria Cross. On that day seven Bostons attacked stores and buildings at Salamaua. Piloting one of the twin engined attackers at minimum altitude was Flt Lt Newton. In the process of putting his bombs on two main enemy fuel dumps which destroyed some 40,000gal of fuel, his Boston took four hits which severely damaged his engines, fuel tanks and structural airframe. Despite the damage, Newton managed to keep the Boston flying the 180 miles back to base.

Two days later he was called on to attack the Japanese installations at Salamaua once more. As he came in at minimum altitude to hit his target, Newton's aircraft was hit and burst into flames. Exhibiting an excellent bit of flying, he managed to get the aircraft on an even keel and head it out to sea where his crew could have a chance of survival. Newton and Sgt J. Lyon came out of the ditching unscathed but Sgt B. G. Eastwood was lost.

The two men made it to shore where they were spotted by other Bostons in the area. Unfortunately, both men were captured by the Japanese the next day, and were taken to Lae for interrogation by enemy forces. There Rear-Admiral Fujita, Commander of the Imperial Naval Forces in the area, ordered Newton to be sent back to Salamaua for execution in accordance with the Samurai Code. There he was beheaded on 29 March

1943. Sgt J. Lyon was also interrogated and was bayoneted to death at Lae.

Throughout the balance of 1943 the limited numbers of A-20s in the South-West Pacific continued to strike out at enemy airfields, supply lines and shipping in support of Allied forces which were slowly working their way up the New Guinea coast.

Reinforcements for A-20 forces began in earnest in January 1944 when the four squadrons of the 3rd Bombardment Group were all converted to A-20s. Following closely in the theatre came the A-20 equipped 312th Bombardment Group which got into combat in February 1944 and the 417th Bombardment Group, also fully equipped with A-20s, flew its first combat mission in March 1944.

Two of the A-20 groups took part in what was to be the mission that all but annihilated the Japanese aerial forces in the Hollandia, New Guinea, area. In preparation for the invasion of Hollandia, the 5th Air Force had previously dispatched their heavy bombers to strike at the three enemy airfields in the area. It was decided that a heavily concentrated raid by all the bomber force that could be mustered was necessary. The general stategy called for the B-24s to come in at high level followed by the A-20s at treetop level dropping their lethal parafrags. The B-25s would follow later to mop up whatever remained.

On 3 April some 65 B-24s escorted by P-38s made the initial strike on the Japanese airfields. Shortly thereafter 96 A-20s of the 3rd and 312th Bombardment Groups came in on the deck. Ground fire was intense but fortunately didn't take a great toll of the attackers. Quite a number of enemy fighter planes took-off to intercept, but the P-38s took care of most of them.

Two days later the A-20s were once more a part of the force that went back to Hollandia to finish the job. The destruction that the bombers wrought on the airfields had a great effect on the invasion of the area by Allied ground forces later in the month. At least 340 Japanese aircraft had been destroyed on the ground. The defeat was such that Lt-Gen Itabana, Commander of the 6th Japanese Air Division, was relieved of his command.

Throughout the summer of 1944 the three A-20s groups carried the war to the enemy's airfields, supply lines, shipping and barge traffic. The A-20 pilots became very proficient at barge busting using delayed fuse bombs to blast the bottoms of the flat bottomed vessels. A number of armament experiments were carried out, some successful, and some not. One that was not successful was Lt-Col 'Pappy' Gunns' inovation of 14 machine guns in the nose of the A-20. Capt Tom Jones of the 312th Group tried it out

Below: A-20s of the 3rd Bombardment Group outbound in formation. In view of their low-level tactics, the 3rd needed no glass-nosed bombardier aircraft. / USAF

Below: This sequence, which is probably one of the most striking ever taken depicting the death of an aircraft, was made on 22 July 1944. The A-20s of the 387th Squadron, 312th Bomb Group struck the Japanese base at Kokas on the Bay of Sekar in Netherlands New Guinea. The aircraft flown by Lt James L. Knarr, who was on his seventh mission, was hit and plunged into the water. There was no chance for Knarr and his gunner S/Sgt Charles C. Reichley to get out. / *USAF*

Right: A veteran of 126 missions with the 388th Bomb Squadron of the 312th Bomb Group was *Miss Pam* whose crew chief was S/Sgt J. S. Wray. / *USAF*

Below: *Little Isadore* a veteran of many missions with the 89th Squadron, 3rd Bomb Group over Hollandia in August 1944. / *USAF*

and stated that when all guns were fired the A-20 all but stalled out, not to speak of the noise it caused aboard the craft. He returned to base and was most vehement in his remarks that the experiment was not successful.

In October 1944 American forces returned to the Philippine Islands, but it was November before the first A-20 group moved to Leyte and December before all three of the units were in the combat area once more. However, the arrival set the stage for what was one of the most spectacular A-20 operations of the war. The mission called for the A-20s of the 312th and 417th Bomb Groups along with the B-25s of the 345th Bomb Group to fly a 6½hr mission covering over 1,000 miles from Leyte to strike Clark Field north of Manila on the island of Luzon. The plan called for two waves of 72 aircraft making line abreast attacks at low level. One wave would fly a north-south route while the other flew from west to east.

The aircraft were airborne on the morning of 7 January 1945, and formed up over Mindoro. Just as the force assembled they sighted the Allied invasion fleet headed for its landing on Lingayen Gulf. At about the same time two Japanese aircraft were sighted and this brought up a terrific barrage from the US Navy. However, the enemy aircraft evaded swiftly, but the US bombers were obliged to take immediate evasive action to keep from being shot down by their own fleet.

On reaching their initial point on the coast of Luzon the force turned inland but there was some confusion when it was found that the pass that the aircraft were to fly through was obscured by low hanging overcast. Slowly, the aircraft began to drop down into the clouds hopeful that they would be able to negotiate their passage safely. Fortunately, all of them did so and as they broke out of the clouds they sighted Clark Field dead ahead,

Below: Another veteran gunship of the 388th Squadron. The heart painted under the horizontal stabiliser designated the 388th Squadron. The 386th Squadron used a club, the 387th a diamond and the 389th a spade. / USAF

completely in the clear. The enemy was caught by surprise when the first wave went in. Some of the anti-aircraft batteries were still covered when the force roared in over the Japanese installations and let go with their machine guns and dropped their parafrags.

The second wave was not quite so fortunate as the Japanese detonated some large explosive charges just as they roared across the field. Three of the A-20s felt their fury and were downed by the explosions. One B-25 fell to anti-aircraft fire and one other A-20 was hit and crashed on the way out. Otherwise, the mission was extremely successful and for all practical purposes Clark Field was lost to the enemy as a base.

As American forces moved forward on the island of Luzon the A-20s continued their support work and in due time moved on to Luzon. During their operations from Luzon in March and April of 1945 the 312th Bombardment Group was awarded a Distinguished Unit Citation for the extraordinary missions that they flew against enemy plants on the island of Formosa that were producing

Far left, top: The destruction wrought by the A-20s is quite evident in this photo of aircraft wrecked by the 312th Bomb Group at Wewak. / *USAF*

Far left, bottom: A-20 of the 389th Bomb Squadron sits amidst the wreckage of Japanese aircraft at Hollandia in August 1944. / *USAF*

Left and below: A-20s of the 312th Bomb Group depart the flaming oil target at Boela on the island of Ceram in a most successful mission on 14 July 1944. / *USAF*

butanol, an important component in aviation gasoline. The A-20s of the 312th each carried six 100lb napalm bombs slung under their wings in addition to their regular bomb loads in striking these targets. Coming in at low level the A-20s rained their destruction on the highly inflammable installations and were successful in completely wrecking this enemy operation.

In August 1945 the A-20 units moved up to Okinawa to provide support to American forces getting ready for the invasion of the main Japanese islands. However, the end of the war prevented most of them from seeing action from their new stations. The 3rd Group begun to receive new A-26s by this time, but when they made their initial strikes at the enemy's homeland on 9 August, there were A-20s in the number.

The reliable old A-20 had come all the way up from the jungles of New Guinea to the Japanese home islands and was still very actively present at the end of World War II in the Pacific.

Left: The many successes of the A-20s in the South-West Pacific would never have been possible without the devoted efforts of the ground crew who worked in the most trying field conditions throughout the war. Here a 3rd Bomb Group crew performs maintenance on an A-20G in the Philippines. / *USAF*

Above: Leaving a smoking target in its wake is an A-20 of the 389th Bomb Squadron, 312th Bomb Group, after a strike on San Jose and San Nicholas in the Philippines on 23 January 1945. / *USAF*

Left: A-20 of the 417th Bomb Group over a smoking target at Latain Point in the Philippines on 9 February 1945. / USAF

Right and below: A-20s sweep in over Clark Field north of Manila on the island of Luzon on 7 January 1945. In the second photo the A-20s have gained altitude and are heading for home after a very successful mission. / USAF

Pacific Gunships
Col Donald Hall

'I joined the 89th Squadron of the 3rd Attack Group in 1941. During this period we received our first Douglas A-20s. At that time our armament consisted of only two .30 calibre machine guns in the nose. Of course, at that time we considered ourselves as bombers, not strafers, so we paid no attention to this. Our primary achievement during this period was learning to fly the A-20 at low altitude in formation and to place our quarter pound flour sack bombs on ground targets. We gained much experience in this type of operation during the Louisiana manoeuvres and other tactical exercises. We became quite adept at hitting our targets and learned to keep the pilot's head on the horizon in low-level formation flying.

'My squadron sailed from the United States for the Pacific Theatre of Operations in January 1942, and we arrived at Brisbane, Australia on 25 February 1942. At this time I was given command of the 89th Squadron which consisted of a relatively small contingent of men and no aeroplanes. I took my

new command up to Townsville at this time, but with no aircraft there was little we could do. Our maintenance men assisted in patching up some of the B-17-Es of the 19th Bombardment Group that were straggling in from the defeat in Java. It was here that I met Paul I. "Pappy" Gunn, who was to become the "Father" of the A-20 gunship. Gunn was a captain at that time and he flew into Townsville piloting a B-17 on three engines. Little did I know then how closely we would work for such a long period of time.

'The 89th never did get any aircraft while we were at Townsville, but I did manage to get in one mission in a B-17 before taking my outfit up to join the rest of the 3rd Group at Charters Towers, Australia, in March 1942.

'At this time the 13th and 90th Squadrons of the 3rd Group began to receive some B-25s that had originally been built for the Dutch. These aircraft had arrived too late for the Java campaign and were shortly put to good use by our sister squadrons. We began to receive a few A-20s, believe it or not, that we

Below: Maj Don Hall (left) and Capt Christian Pietre, two of the pioneer pilots of the gunships in the South-West Pacific. / *USAF*

Above: An A-20 of the 89th Bomb Squadron laying a smoke screen in 1942. Note that the red ball is still in the national insignia. / D. Hall

Left: *Cactus Don* the A-20 flown by Maj Don Hall. While flying the gunships Hall had the distinction of downing several Japanese aircraft with his nose guns. / D. Hall

Above: *Little Joe* a veteran of 127
missions with the 312th Bomb
Group. / *USAF*

had previously flown in the States. The
aircraft as reassembled were equipped with
four forward-firing .30 calibre machine guns
which was still a light load for combat
operations. However, the primary drawback
at this stage was the lack of range of the A-20.
This was vastly improved with the installation of a 450gal fuel tank in the forward
bomb bay. To offset the loss in bomb load
that the fuel tank installation brought about,
"Pappy" Gunn undertook to make the A-20
a real strafer. He installed four .50 calibre
machine guns in the nose where the bombardier would normally sit. This made the
aircraft a bit nose heavy but installation of
some weight in the rear took care of this.

'To increase further our effectiveness work
was being done to convert the standard 23lb
fragmentation bombs to parafrags. This
innovation consisted of installation of an
instantaneous fuse and small parachutes
attached to the tail fins of the bombs. This
would allow us to drop a bevy of these
missiles on enemy targets at extremely low
altitude and still have time to clear the area
before the bombs began exploding.

'We did a lot of hard work while we were at
Charters Towers. Day after day we practised
formation flying, bombing and strafing. We
also knew that with the lack of fighter aircraft
in the theatre to give us escort we would have
to fly a lot of missions at night. Before we left
Charters Towers we became very proficient
at flying formation and navigating at night.

'When we moved up to Kila Kila (Three-
Mile Drome) outside of Port Moresby, New
Guinea, in August 1942 we were ready for
combat. At the time of our arrival the Japanese
had occupied Buna on the north side of New
Guinea and their ground forces were advan-
cing up the Kokoda Trail across the Owen
Stanley Mountains towards Port Moresby.
At the same time, another Japanese column
was advancing down the northern coast of
New Guinea towards Milne Bay located on
the southern tip of New Guinea. By the end
of August, Australian troops had stalled the
advance on Milne Bay, but the fight along the
Kokoda Trail still raged and the fate of Port
Moresby hung in the balance.

'Although they were not all in commission,
we managed to assemble 13 A-20s at Port
Moresby by the end of August 1942. On 31
August we got our first combat mission
underway. I was to lead six A-20s which
would strafe the Lae airfield after Martin
B-26s had bombed it. Our formation arrived
at the target in time to see the B-26s releasing
their fragmentation bombs from an altitude
of 10,000ft.

'Then we went in on the deck to strafe the
airfield. We caught the Japanese completely
by surprise. The concentrated firepower that
we had in the nose really worked well against
their aircraft and anti-aircraft installations.
We were so low that we could see the sur-
prised expressions on the faces of the men as
we swept over them. There were a few enemy

Above: A-20s of the 417th Group lined on the runway following their move to Noemfoor in September 1944. / USAF

fighters in the air, but none of our aircraft were damaged to any extent and all returned home safely.

'The mission initiated a tactic that we would use successfully many times. Sometimes we would precede the medium bombers with our strafing and at other times we would follow them in. It kept the enemy guessing and kept his anti-aircraft gunners with their heads down because they were always looking for a second wave and didn't know what altitude the attack would come from.

'At this time we were also kept quite busy attacking the Japanese advancing along the Kokoda Trail. It was very difficult to locate the enemy under the jungle curtain as we flew up and down the mountain canyons. Some of the roughest missions I ever flew were those on which we attempted to find and attack the enemy at night along the trail. Sighting a pinpoint of light and keeping away from the canyon walls was quite an ordeal.

'On 5 September 1942 I led 16 A-20s which were escorted by 26 Bell P-400s to Buna. The weather was quite bad and we had to dodge in and out of cloud formations all the way. This time there was no surprise. The anti-aircraft boys were waiting for us. However, we dropped down to low level and did our strafing bit which destroyed a number of aircraft. We did observe that a number of the enemy aircraft that had been reported on the ground turned out to be dummies made of wood and fabric. That was another advan-

tage of low-level work. There was no way to fool us with camouflage.

'I led a formation of 15 A-20s back to Buna on the afternoon of 11 September. Once more, we had to skirt bad weather en route to the target, but this time when we arrived we caught them by surprise. This time we flew a coordinated strafing pattern, with Capt Christian Pietre leading one formation and I led the other.

'On my first pass I caught a truckload of Japanese troops on the runway and caught them with a full burst from the nose guns. As I came back on the second pass I caught a Zero that had just taken-off in a tight turn. I didn't know that I could catch him but I pulled my nose around, gave him a burst from the eight nose guns and he immediately cartwheeled into the ground.

'After we had expended our ammunition we set course for home, skirting bad weather all the way. All of the A-20s, save one, returned to base safely. The missing aircraft managed to crash land about 30 miles from base and the crew was saved.

'On 12 September we flew our first parafrag missions that were to prove so successful against ground targets. My nine A-20s were to fly low and drop their parafrags and the Martin B-26s would follow us in. The weather was bad, as usual, and we came in through the rain. We let down over the sea and attacked at an altitude of 60-70ft. Just as we came in over the airfield I sighted two

81

Right: *Kay* undergoes maintenance at its new base at Noemfoor. Note that the ground crew is being forced to use boxes for lack of maintenance stands. / *USAF*

Below: Head-on view of a 3rd Bomb Group A-20 showing the skull painted on the nose of the aircraft. Note two gun ports protruding through the eyes. / *USAF*

Zeroes taking-off. They commenced to break, but I put a burst into one of them and put him into the trees. We proceeded to drop our bombs and make continued strafing passes. On the third pass we had just about everything burning.

'As I came off the target I received a call on the radio that informed me that I had one engine smoking badly. I knew that I would never get over the Owen Stanelys with a bad engine so I had to swing far to the south and proceed home from there. Regardless, we had a most successful mission and were credited with the destruction of 17 enemy aircraft.

'Another big show for us took place on 1 November. The plan called for the B-25s to strike the airfield at Lae first. They were to be followed by B-26s and we were to come in about half an hour later to get at the Japanese fighters coming in to land after intercepting the earlier strikes at medium altitude.

'We took off with 14 A-20s with a half dozen P-40s to act as escort. There were a lot of clouds and we became separated from the P-40s en route to the target. Upon arrival at the rendezvous, we waited but the B-26s never put in an appearance. We flew on up the coast of New Guinea and let down for our bombing and strafing runs. Capt Pietre was to lead six A-20s making their runs from south to north while I was to lead eight aircraft making runs from north to south. As we came in on the target we spotted 20 Japanese fighters overhead. They saw us about the

same time and dived down to attack us on our runs. I had a long run and I could hear the machine guns of our rear gunners blazing away as the Zeroes attacked from the rear. They made their pass at us and pulled up into Immelmans to come back at us.

'At this time I saw the P-40s engaging some of the Japanese fighters off to my right, but then I sighted a Zero coming back at me head-on. I hit the gun tit and watched my slugs tear into him. One of his wings seemed to tear off and he went by streaming flames.

'A number of our A-20s had been hit in the attack and we all headed for cloud cover to escape the enemy fighters. One of our aircraft had to land at 7-Mile Airdrome due to his damage, but the rest of us made it home safely.

'We had learned on these early missions that we couldn't knock out the Japanese airfields by bombing them for they were all dirt runways and it only took a short while to fill the craters in. However, we had learned that the strafing and parafrag attacks were very effective in knocking out the enemy's aircraft on the ground. The gun nose of the A-20 was quite lethal and other field modifications were used with great effect. One of these was the installation of steel armour plating under the seats for further protection of the crew while on the low-level strikes.

'All in all the A-20 was a very effective weapon in the South-West Pacific and it remained so throughout the war.'

Below: Making one of the low-level passes for which it was famous, an A-20 passed over a Japanese 'Betty' bomber at Lae, New Guinea. / *USAF*

The Battle of the Bismarck Sea

Early 1943 found the Japanese doing their utmost to hold onto their bases in New Guinea. When the Australians began construction of an airbase at Wau, some 40 miles south-west of Lae, they immediately reinforced their garrison at Lae. In mid-January they successfully landed an additional 10,000 troops at Wewak, to the north. General Imamura, commander of the Japanese Eighteenth Army, decided in February that it was imperative that the garrison at Lae be reinforced substantially to counter the Australian base further.

It was decided that a troop convoy would be assembled in the harbour at Rabaul, the Japanese bastion on New Britain, to deliver some 6,900 men to Lae. This entailed an exposed troop movement of over 260 miles along the northern coast of New Britain and south through the Vitiaz Straits to Lae. The Japanese planned to use bad weather as a cover for the convoy as much as possible and to employ their land based fighters to the utmost to provide top cover for the convoy. On 28 February 1943, the convoy, consisting of six transports escorted by eight destroyers left Rabaul. The weather was very bad and the Japanese had great hopes for the convoy to make the dash to Lae undiscovered. Alas, their luck did not hold out for they were spotted by an American B-24 Liberator bomber on 1 March.

The US Army Air Force's Fifth Air Force immediately began to formulate plans to strike out at the convoy. A primary and vital component of the strike against the enemy ships was to be the veteran A-20 89th Squadron now commanded by Capt Glenn W. Clark. This is Clark's story of the 89th part of the Bismarck Sea operation:

'We were apparently a vital part of the proposed Bismarck Sea operation due to our training in skip bombing. This tactic had apparently been instituted by the B-17s

Below: Capt Glenn W. Clark who led the 89th Squadron on its historic strike in the Battle of the Bismarck Sea is shown (left) with his crew. / *USAF*

which had done some work in attempting to skip their bombs into shipping targets flying at night at an altitude of about 1,000ft.

'No one ever told the 89th Squadron to learn skip bombing. As we took-off from our base at Kila Kila we would often test our forward firing guns on an old burned out ship hulk just off the coast. Our early missions had been primarily concerned with dropping parafrags on airfields, but some of the pilots got the idea that we just might get the opportunity to strike shipping some day, so they began to load the A-20s with 100lb "blue devils" and practise skipping them into the side of the old burned out ship on the coast. After a time a number of our pilots became quite proficient at it.

'In late February our intelligence sources reported that the Japanese were putting together a convoy at Rabaul which would probably be sent to reinforce their garrisons at either Wewak or Lae. We knew no further details of this until on the afternoon of 2 March when 5th ADVON (5th Air Force Advanced Echelon) called on us inquiring as to our capability of flying a last light mission against the convoy. It requested that we (the 89th Squadron) lead a mission by the entire 5th Air Force against the ships. The weather was bad with a lot of thunder-storm activity. The A-20 was not famous for its bad weather capability and to make a low-level strike at last light and get back to our staging base at Dobadura was not favourably considered. We told ADVON what we thought of the chances and apparently they went along with us. However, they did send out the B-17s and B-24s to bomb from high altitude. They managed to find the convoy and were able to do some damage late that afternoon.

'Actually the A-20s took a chance, so to speak, by not going on the evening of 2 March for if the convoy had been headed for Wewak, it would have been out of our range by the next morning.

'Such was not the case, and next morning we loaded each of the 12 A-20s that would fly the mission with two 500lb bombs. The plan called for two aircraft to attack each of the six transports in the convoy. As leader I would pick out a ship in the middle of the convoy. leaving the ships on either side for my element leaders. Our attack was to be made at minimum altitude with one bomb to be dropped slightly ahead of the ship and one right into the side. This would give us two skip bombs and two point blank bombs in each transport.

Right: The mast top strikes at the Battle of the Bismarck Sea must have been very similar to this strike on a Japanese freighter off New Guinea. / *USAF*

'My orders were to form my 12 A-20s in formation over Cape Ward Hunt. There we would rendezvous with the B-25s of the 90th Squadron and we would follow them to the target. Upon our arrival at the rendezvous point there were several B-25 units in the area and I had to make a decision as to which was the 90th Squadron under the lead of their commander – Capt Ed Larner. I finally picked the low group and fortunately this proved to be the 90th Squadron.

'I didn't know exactly where the convoy was supposed to be but we had no trouble finding them. As we sighted their wakes I noted that the escort destroyers immediately broke into a protective circle around the transports just like the old wild west wagons going all out for protection from the Indians.

'The original plan called for the B-17s and B-24s to go in first from high altitude. They were to be followed by B-25s which would strike from medium altitudes. The B-25s of the 90th Squadron and our A-20s were to swing around to the north of the convoy and fly our attacks at mast head coming south. This would serve not only to confuse the enemy, but if any of our aircraft were hit it would be headed home.

'We approached the convoy, still following the B-25s of the 90th Squadron. I sighted a large Japanese destroyer steaming in the opposite direction from our course and then suddenly I saw it disappear in a cloud of black smoke. Ed Larner apparently took the destruction of the destroyer as a gap in the protective circle around the transports and headed right in rather than continue our route arond the convoy to the north. I decided to follow him in with my A-20s.

'I passed in front of a destroyer which began shooting at us and lined up on a transport. I then noted that Capt Ed Chudoba, was headed for the same ship. I decided to go ahead with my attack on the same ship. I dropped my bombs as planned and saw one of them go right into the side of the ship.

'In the confusion of the attack my A-20s didn't follow the original plan. Some of them dropped one bomb on one ship and the second on another. Capt Beck strafed a transport when he couldn't get his bombs to drop.

'I continued on to the north towards Finschafen and en route I saw splashes begin to appear in the water. I had an idea that this must be from bombs the heavies were dropping at high altitude. I lined up on one of the transports for a strafing run but about that time I sighted an Australian Beaufighter start his strafing run on the same ship. I decided that in such a confused issue I would be better off to pull up to the left and get out of the area before I wound up shooting up somebody or getting shot up myself.

'Surprisingly, all of the A-20s came off the target and formed up for the run home. We all made it back safely and went in for debriefing. We knew that we had made a number of hits on the ships of the convoy and that our attack had been quite successful. However, I didn't learn until several days later that 80% of our bombs had been direct hits.'

Bad weather prevented the A-20s from going back to the convoy that afternoon but some of the B-25s and heavy bombers rained further destruction on the surviving ships of the enemy force.

The following day B-17s attacked the remnants of the convoy once more. All six transports and four of the Japanese destroyers were sunk in the Battle of the Bismarck Sea which was to prove one of the war's greatest victories by aircraft of the US Fifth Air Force and the Royal Australian Air Force. Of the nearly 6,000 Japanese troops on the transports en route to Lae, the surviving destroyers were able to save only 2,700. The A-20s of the 89th Squadron were surely responsible for the destruction of a large share of the men and transports in this ill-fated Japanese convoy.

Far left: Gunship comes in to roost at Dobodura, New Guinea, on 8 January 1944. The aircraft belonged to the 90th Squadron of the 3rd Bomb Group. / USAF

Below: A-20 of the 3rd Bomb Group being fitted with rocket tubes in late June 1944. Note the 20mm cannon installed in the nose rather than the conventional .50 calibres. / USAF

The P-70 in the South-West Pacific

Lt Col Curtis R. Ehlert USAF (Ret)

'After a short tour with the 18th Fighter Control Squadron during July and August of 1942, all of the enlisted men who had attended radar school at Morrison Field, Florida, were notified that they were being transferred to the 6th Fighter Squadron. The 6th had just received 25 Douglas P-70s and we were called into the squadron to operate and maintain the radar equipment of these night fighters.

'Our training in night fighter equipment had consisted of viewing a British training film barely explaining the concept of operation, ie how we could detect and track airborne targets with the AI (airborne interception) gear. On the 5 September 1942, I became a member of the 6th Squadron at Kuhuku Field at the extreme northern tip of the island of Oahu, Hawaii.

'Besides maintaining and operating the AI equipment, the people who had attended radar school were going to be used as a training nucleus for other personnel in the squadron. We were told that armourers, aircraft mechanics and radio mechanics were to be trained as airborne radar operators. This really wasn't met with any enthusiasm by the radar people.

'However, we were all given flight physicals and started flying in the P-70s. During this period we usually went up in flights of two aircraft and used each other as target and interceptor during the flying period. A point that is important here is that we had to make up our own pilot-operator commentary. We had seen that the British had used the terms "port" and "starboard" for the turn commands in one training film and by copying some of the terms we were able to set up a standardised commentary. Although it became apparent later, even though we would always fly with the same pilot, we wanted everyone in the squadron on the same general footing. A "gentle port" or "gentle starboard" was a 10° bank; "port" or "starboard" was a 20° bank, etc. This method of directing the pilot seemed like a relatively simple and yet an effective system and with a little practice a radar operator would direct a pilot to within a visual sighting of the target even on the darkest night. We were convinced that we would always be able to see the exhaust pattern of the engines and then visually shoot the plane down.

'Many of the pilots were not too enthusiastic about flying P-70s. The squadron had been equipped with P-40s prior to the Pearl Harbor attack and they all wanted back in day fighters.

'In November 1942, we moved to Kipapa Gulch, just below Wheeler Field and started pulling night alert with the P-70s. Shortly after our arrival Lt Robert Sugnet of the Signal Corps was assigned to our squadron as a radar officer. He had been to England and had observed and worked with RAF night fighters. His experience with the RAF and his technical knowledge of the equipment gave us a tremendous boost as we were subjects of the "blind leading the blind" up to this point.

'In January 1943, Maj Wharton selected six crews and 18 other maintenance people for a detachment that was to be deployed to the South-West Pacific. The Marines had landed on Guadalcanal in August 1942 and were being bombed almost nightly by the Japanese.

'During this period we started learning a bit about aerial gunnery. In addition to the four fixed 20mm cannon on the P-70 it was fitted with a pair of .30 calibre machine guns to fire out of the opened rear cockpit and a single .50 calibre gun was installed to fire out of the lower access hatch. Just what good these guns were going to be on a night fighter we never figured out.

'It would also appear that the person making the decision to deploy us to a combat area was unaware of the fact that we as a night fighter squadron could not operate autonomously, but were completely dependent upon ground radar or ground directed instructions to get into a fairly close proximity (within two miles) of the target aircraft before our airborne equipment would be effective.

'On 18 February 1943, we departed for Guadalcanal with six P-70s and two LB-30s. After an arduous journey through squalls and extended distances during which one P-70 was lost without a trace, we arrived at

Guadalcanal on 28 February. We had nightly raids from the Japanese and one day raid. Either Guadalcanal or Tugagi would be bombed. We could see the anti-aircraft fire at the bombers and could see the fires that were started. "Washing Machine Charlie" would sit over the island in the searchlights as the 90mm guns would blast away. It always seemed that the aircraft were just out of range in height. They would be over the island for 30 minutes to an hour, occasionally dropping a bomb. These raids, although they didn't do too much damage certainly irritated the troops and prevented them from getting a good night's sleep. Of course, nobody could understand why the black night fighters didn't scramble when "Charlie" came over.

'During the second week of March our little detachment moved off of Henderson up to Carney Field, near Koli Point. This was the field that we would use as a base of operations after the ground radar station was completed.

'Our main task consisted of digging trenches for the antenna counterpoise for the radio transmitter. The counterpoise was an effective ground for the antenna and consisted of copper wires buried in the sand and emanating from the base of the antenna like spokes in a bicycle wheel. The radiating element of the antenna would be insulated from the ground or the counterpoise and fed at the base. The antenna was set on a Coca-Cola bottle, guyed at 120° increments and proved to be quite effective. I often wonder how many people knew that the entire success of a Ground Control Intercept station depended on the strength of an empty Coca-Cola bottle.

'The radar station, aptly given the call sign "Kiwi", was finally completed and we flew a few flights to assist in the calibration of the ground station and from all appearances were ready for business. This particular airborne-ground system was being committed in a combat area and operated by people who had absolutely no or very little experience. The aircrews had never practised this and I doubt seriously if the controllers on the ground had any experience in controlling airborne intercepts. Where the English had used radar, sound and visual inputs to a combat operations centre where the information had been correlated and plotted on a table, our controllers were going to control directly from the information on the scope.

'We started pulling alert at Carney Field on 25 March 1943 with five crews and two crews on alert each night. One crew would take from 6pm until midnight and the second from midnight to 6am.

'Most of the crews were anxious to get at "Charlie" and in the first couple of weeks several got close, but nobody had any success. "Charlie" changed his tactics a bit. Instead of staying in the lights over the island, he would occasionally try to sneak in just before dawn or at dusk and consequently we started flying patrols during that period.

'Because there wasn't any single defence command or commander, all defence forces operated as separate units. The night fighters with their ground station, the anti-aircraft batteries with their 90mm. If the Japanese were in the searchlights the 90mm fired at them without regard for friendly fighters in the area.

'On 19 April, Lt Bennett and Cpl Ed Tomlinson flew through the 90mm anti-aircraft fire to get a Japanese Betty bomber right over the airfield. You could see the tracers leave the P-70 and then watch the Betty explode. All the people on the ground clapped and cheered and hollered when they saw the bomber explode. It was quite a sight.

'Our P-70 went after enemy aircraft on two more nights during May but met with no success. However, P-38s were successful on these occasions.

'This proved to be the beginning of the end of the P-70 on Guadalcanal. The pilots of the 6th Squadron were given P-38s. The P-70 just wasn't the plane for this particular job. We couldn't make a high altitude night fighter out of a low altitude attack bomber loaded with four 20mm cannon and a radar set. We tried stripping the P-70s to get more altitude but this didn't make an appreciable difference. We had one up to 29,000ft but the plane was just hanging on the props.'

Below: A Douglas P-70 night fighter as described by Curtis Ehlert of the 6th Night Fighter Squadron. Note the radar antenna and the gun installations.
/ T. K. Lewis

Ditching an A-20G

Lt Norman J. Summers

'Taking off from Kornasoren airfield at Noemfoor on 1 October 1944 with the 674th Bombardment Squadron in a formation of 12 A-20s led by a B-25, I was flying number three in the second box of the formation. My turret gunner was S/Sgt Robert F. Evans.

'The assigned target for that day was Langgoer Aerodrome, Kai Islands and was to be bombed by the 13 aircraft from medium altitude. During the entire flight to the target, my A-20 performed perfectly, and just prior to the target run the formation tightened up on the lead B-25, and evasive action was taken. As I opened my bomb bay doors, the first bursts of flak appeared to the right of and at the same altitude. The formation made a gentle turn to the left and several bursts of flak appeared on the original course. Another turn was made to the right and flak began to burst all around the formation. Several bursts appeared between the flight leader's aircraft and my own, causing the A-20 to shake slightly from the concussions.

'Upon completion of the target run, the formation made a steep diving turn to the right and I was again jarred violently by two bursts of flak, just off my left wing. It shook the aircraft so severely that I thought it had been hit but could not ascertain the extent of the damage due to the violence of the evasive action. Sgt Evans called on the interphone and reported "Bombs away". and that the last bursts of flak had jarred loose quite a bit of the equipment in the gunner's compartment but that it all had been replaced.

'Levelling off at about 5,500ft, the formation took a heading of approximately 65 degrees on course toward Kornasoren airfield. The left engine of my aircraft began to cut-out and run roughly. I looked out and saw a hole approximately 10 inches in diameter in the lower part of the left engine cowling also one, about four inches in diameter in the leading edge of the left wing. I immediately looked to the right side and in the right wing there was a hole running diagonally through the leading edge approximately four inches long and three quarters of an inch across. When my left engine began to cut out, I broke away from the formation as I could not keep up at that rate of speed and I tried all my controls in order to try to remedy the trouble. After changing my throttle setting, mixture control, RPM, and manifold pressure, I found that by pulling 22in of mercury, 1,800rpm, full rich mixture and using the left booster pump, that the engine would run much smoother. Just as I remedied the trouble in the left engine, the right engine began to miss and also started to shoot out flame and oil. I immediately put the mixture control to emergency rich and turned on the right booster pump and the engine smoothed out. (Later I learned that it continued to throw flame and oil.) While I was changing my throttle settings I lost another 1,500ft of altitude, but levelled off and was able to maintain an air speed of 185mph for approximately 15min, and began to feel that it was possible to make it back to Kornasoren.

'The left engine finally cut out entirely and no matter what I did it would not start. I feathered the propeller and proceeded on single engine, loosing some altitude, I immediately contacted Sgt Evans and told him to prepare to ditch. Channel "C" was the only channel operative on VHF at this time and he said that he was going to jettison every piece of loose equipment and prepare himself for ditching and asked for further instructions as to the ditching procedure.

'Since it had always been my belief that if the gunner would climb in the turret, chop off the dome of the turret to use as an escape hatch, fasten the safety belt, that his chances for survival would be greater upon ditching. I so instructed Sgt Evans and his successful escape seems to bear out my theory. He and I had gone over this method of ditching prior to take-off.

'As preparations were being made to ditch, the plane continued to fly on the right engine and was loosing altitude slowly. I did not worry about the loss of altitude, until I approached the mainland and then I realised that the mountain range ahead could not be climbed. Soon after crossing on to the mainland the right engine cut out and I tried to start it but all my efforts were in vain, and I feathered the propeller immediately. I then called Sgt Evans and told him to be ready to ditch. I tried to pull the emergency hatch release but it would not work.

'I was then over the southern tip of Dutch New Guinea and about 40 miles south-west of the enemy base at Utarom. I made the final approach with full flaps at 140mph to the north, paralleling the coast, just north of Adi Island and the Nautilus Straits. As the aircraft approached the water and just before the impact I heard the right propeller tip, slightly tick the tops of the waves, but was able to make the correction and started to skim the tail along the top of the water. I kept the stick pulled back as far as I could, into my stomach, and then the nose burrowed into the water with a hell of a bang and it felt as though I had hit a stone wall.

'Since the emergency hatch release did not work I had to open the canopy by hand. The plane immediately began to sink with a gurgling noise, and struggling free from my crash harness, I started to climb out but something, which I decided later was my parachute, caught on the bucket seat pulled me back into the water. I was able to get a deep breath before submerging into the water. I freed myself and pitched the life raft over board. I came to the surface of the water but I still had my parachute on and I rolled over with my head under water and again had to struggle before I was able to free myself and come to the surface.

'I remember that all this time I had a hard time seeing and it seemed as if there was a haze over my eyes and it was not until later that I found that I had head lacerations and was bleeding badly. I inflated my life jacket and then noticed Sgt Evans paddling toward me and we both managed to inflate the raft and found that with teamwork it was a comparatively easy job. Sgt Evans climbed aboard and I was able to get about half way in but could not go any further, until he helped me in. I, then became nauseated and passed out for about an hour. Sgt Evans told me that I was talking to him all the time and that he had given me first aid and bandaged me with his silk map.

'When I came to I asked Sgt Evans about his condition and he told me that his right leg was broken. I looked him over and saw his leg was badly broken as it was dangling and bleeding at the shin. I gave him one-half grain of morphine in his left arm, a dose of sulfadiazine inwardly, and dusted the open wound where the bone had broken through the skin, with sulfadiazine. I tried to find something that could be used as a splint and finally took a life vest, partially inflated it and wrapped it around his leg as a splint.

'Settling in the life raft as comfortably as possible, I opened the emergency ration kit. We then shared a chocolate bar and some water from it. During this time two of the squadron's aircraft were circling over the raft and occasionally came down to buzz us.

'One of the aircraft left and then finally, the remaining one gave us a buzz and waggled his wings and took off toward our airfield. At about 1715 hours a Catalina was sighted coming from the north and as it was becoming slightly dark, I tried to break open the emergency flare kit, but was unable to do so because the webbing over the flares was wet and had shrunk. I didn't have a knife and I broke two finger nails in the process of tearing the webbing loose. Sgt Evans put out some sea dye marker but before a flare could be fired the Catalina passed over the raft and did not show any signs of sighting it.

'About 15 minutes later three A-20s passed approximately three miles to the north of the raft, and I immediately fired three flares, but they continued on course. I fired one more flare and then both Sgt Evans and I started to pray that they would see it and come back. Obviously they did see that flare because they came back and gave one hell of a buzz job. The feeling was much too great to express, to know that the aircraft had sighted the flares and that our prayers had been answered.

'Two of the aircraft continued to circle us, one headed in the same direction that the Catalina was last sighted. The Catalina finally returned with the A-20 leading it toward the two circling aircraft at about 6,000ft. The A-20 was flying with wheels down in order to lead the Catalina over the location.

'The Catalina landed and taxied in the direction of the raft and I fired the last flare to direct him to us. The Catalina came to the raft, but I missed the throwline and the flying boat drifted away and lost sight of the raft in the dark. I immediately stood up and started to flash the signal lamp which led the Catalina back again to our position and again they lost us, due to the oncoming darkness. On the third approach the pilot of the Catalina dived off the wing with a throwline fastened to his waist and caught the raft. The raft was pulled up to the Catalina and swung under the tail and was eventually made fast to the port side gun nacelle. A ladder was lowered and I climbed up and as I entered the plane I looked down and Sgt Evans was trying to climb up the ladder with a broken leg. Crew members helped him up the ladder.'

Dogfight in an A-20

Milton W. Johnson

'On 1 October 1944, one A-20 type aircraft of the 417th Bombardment Group, after being hit by flak over Langgoer airfield (New Guinea) ditched at 132°59′ E, 4°8′ S. The crew was reported by a member of the flight to be in a life raft at 133°5′ E, 4°7′ S. The two locations were about 35 miles apart – the correct location was known at the time of take-off.

'At approximately 1500 hours, I took-off along with Maj C. W. Johnson and Maj R. P. Klein in three A-20s to assist in rescue operations. After flying out almost to Mios Waar Island, communications were finally established with a Catalina (Daylight 30) on the common fighter frequency. The fighter grid that I carried and the one carried by Daylight 30 did not agree for some reason, so it was necessary to rendezvous with the Catalina and direct him to the scene of the crash.

'After requesting Daylight 30's position I was informed by the pilot that he was approximately 35 miles south-west of Mios Waar Island. We proceeded to Roon Island and attemped to sight Daylight 30 after getting

his ETA as 15min over Roon Island at 4,500ft. Radio contact was made once again with him, and the pilot explained that he had locations mixed up and that he would be over Mios Waar Island at approximately 4,000ft in about 10min. Fifteen minutes later we sighted the Catalina over Mios Waar Island and directed the Catalina to fly on a heading of approximately 210°. Radio contact was kept with Daylight 30 with the A-20s circling around him as he proceeded to the west end of Adi Island, whereupon he was informed that the crew was down on the coast of New Guinea approximately 10 miles west of the channel between Adi Island and New Guinea. The three A-20s then dropped down to an altitude of approximately 200ft – I was leading with Maj Johnson approximately 300ft out and to the rear on my left wing and Maj Klein was trailing at approximately half a mile.

'Just as Maj Johnson and I started to round Cape Papisoi on a heading of approximately 220° a Japanese float-plane ("Jake") stooged out at about 500ft on an easterly heading and ran just in front of Maj Johnson who was just to the left of me and slightly ahead. The Japanese pilot sighted his A-20 and immediately executed a 180° turn to the right as his rear gunner fired at Maj Johnson's plane. Maj Johnson attempted to fire, assuming that his guns were charged prior to take-off; but they were not, so he pulled around in a 90° turn to the left. The Japanese pilot was just coming out of his turn when Maj Klein started firing from a five o'clock position. I then flew across and above the "Jake", missing it with a short burst after sighting the red roundels on the wings and fuselage. I then pulled up in an abbreviated chandelle to the right after passing over the enemy aircraft. I noticed that Maj Klein had scored a hit in the right wing section which had left a trail of gasoline or smoke. It was then necessary for him to break away to the left. Coming out of the top of my chandelle, I rolled into a diving attack from an eight o'clock position and lined up the "Jake" as he was skidding and diving in evasive action at about 200ft altitude. The first long burst that I fired entered his right wing section and exploded his fuel tank which left a long trail of fire and

black smoke. I applied a little left rudder then, and brought all six .50s to bear on the rear gunner's and pilot's section of the aircraft. My guns were held in this position until it was necessary to pull up over him to prevent collision. Skidding over to the right and looking downward, I saw the "Jake" crash into the water leaving pieces of pontoons approximately 100ft short of where the rest of the aircraft hit on its nose and exploded shooting flames high into the air and leaving gasoline burning on the water with a high column of smoke going upward. One more pass was made by Maj Klein and myself in which we strafed the wreckage.

'The "Jake" crashed head-on into the water at an estimated speed of 170mph and I believe that the entire crew was killed by my machine gun fire prior to the plane's crashing. The whole episode lasted only about one minute and the "Jake" was far inferior to the A-20s in speed and could only slip and·skid in an attempt to get away while the A-20s had to pull out to the side for making passes in order to keep from overrunning him. The "Jake" was shot down at 1730 hours.

'After leaving the scene of the fight, I called Daylight 30 and told him to return home that we were giving up the search until the following day as darkness was approaching and we were confronted with climbing over the mountains which were covered by solid overcast in some places with tops at 8,000ft.

'After releasing Daylight 30 from the mission and starting homeward with Maj Klein on my right wing and Maj Johnson on my left, I saw two red lights about 20 miles to my right and about 10 miles to sea. After turning slightly to the right and then believing them to be navigational aids for Japanese shipping, I again started homeward since these lights appeared 35-40 miles from the reported location of the crew we were seeking. Turning back homeward and keeping my eyes on the location of the red lights, a third one was sighted which gave me the idea that it might be a red flare. Although anxious to start back over the range before total darkness, I decided to establish the indentity of the red lights or flares. I led the other two A-20s back to the scene and flying low sighted the life raft with two missing crew members. Leaving Maj Johnson and Maj Klein with the life raft, I headed back toward Cape Papasoi to try to locate Daylight 30. I attempted to establish radio contact with him, but could not and finally sighted him high overhead and climbed up at the rate of 2,000ft/min to an altitude of 6,500ft to get him back down to effect the rescue. Daylight 30 was unable to understand me on the radio, and after flying close to him and pointing downward and making several attempts I failed to make clear my desires, I decided as a last resort to fly formation with him and lead him to the life raft. I pulled up on his left wing, lowered my landing gear and full flaps, and decreased my airspeed to 150mph. I succeeded in getting him to let down with me in formation and led him to the location were the two other A-20s were circling the life raft. Several circles were made by all three A-20s and the Catalina in an attempt to sight the life raft in semi-darkness. Finally Maj Johnson put us on to him and we kept buzzing the raft making abrupt pull-ups until the Catalina sighted him and made a landing for rescue.'

Below: *Roff Rider* the A-20G flown by Lt-Col M. W. Johnson, CO of the 417th Bomb Group.
/ *M. W. Johnson*

The Spirit of Youth

Nose markings from A-20s of the 312th Bombardment Group in the
South-West Pacific. / *USAF*

The A-26 Invader

The Douglas Aircraft Company undertook design on a new attack bomber in January 1941. It chose to take the better characteristics of the A-20 and incorporate them into a new light bomber the would possess better range, greater speed and heavier armament and bomb load. To meet the three specific needs of the day the Douglas engineers came up with three versions of the aircraft. These were: a light bombardment aircraft with a glass nose; a heavily armed 'gun fighter' with forward-firing cannon and machine guns; and a night fighter version.

The new machine, designated A-26, was an all-metal mid-wing monoplane powered by two R-2800 engines. It incorporated a laminar flow wing and possessed dual-slotted, electrically operated flaps which extended outward and downward, creating greater lift and drag than conventional flaps.

The prototype XA-26-DE was flown on 10 July 1942. It possessed a glass nose and was equipped with two .50 calibre guns mounted on the starboard side of the fuselage and with twin gun installations in remotely controlled dorsal and ventral targets. The

bomb bay was large enough to accommodate 3,000lb of bombs and another 2,000lb could be fitted on four racks beneath the wing outer panels.

The original night fighter design was basically the same as the prototype, but it possessed a solid nose and was to have possessed four 20mm cannon fitted into a ventral tray beneath the fuselage. In view of the performance of the Northrop P-61 of the day, the night fighter version of the A-26 was never put into production.

The original solid nose A-26 was fitted with a 75mm cannon. However, when the A-26 went into production it possessed a six-gun nose with provision for gun tubes to be fitted under the outboard wing panels. Four of these early A-26Bs were sent to the Pacific for combat testing where they were found most unsatisfactory. The two main deficiencies were poor cockpit visibility and insufficient forward-firing armament. Armament was stepped up with provision for guns to be mounted in the wings rather than in drag producing tubes. A redesigned canopy of a 'clam shell' type which vastly improved visibility and general combat effectiveness.

The A-26 saw its first action in Europe (ETO) with the 553rd Squadron of the 386th Bombardment Group. There the aircraft was used at medium altitude and aircrews were very enthusiastic about it. Its range was much greater than that of the A-20, its bomb load was greater and it was much faster. The ETO reception to the aircraft was such that the A-26 began to re-equip A-20 units of the 9th Air Force in November 1944. The first to receive the Invader was the 416th Bombardment Group. Initially there were no A-26Cs with the bombardier glass nose available for them so the solid-nosed A-26Bs had to be led by A-20Ks. The 409th Group began to go into action with A-26s in January 1945 and on one of its missions it was still proven that even with the swift A-26, extreme low altitude was not the way to carry out tactical air operations in the ETO.

The mission on 23 January 1945 called for a strike on enemy transport immobilised on a road between Dasburg and Arzfeld in Belgium. Six A-26s were despatched on the bombing and low-level strafing sweep carrying M-81 fragmentation bombs. Rendezvous was made with the P-51s which were to lead

the way to the target. The fighters spotted the target and set up for the attack. The A-26s proceeded to take up attack formation of three elements of two aircraft, diving to make the attack on the target.

The Invader pilots opened up on the vehicles choking the highway with their nose guns as they went in on the bomb run. Once the bombs had been despatched the Invaders returned to strafe once more. Fire from the ground was devastating. One A-26 was hit and crash landed some seven miles from the target. One of its crew members reported seeing another A-26 hit and cartwheeling into the outskirts of a town where it blew up. Three other A-26s were last seen in the target area. Five out of six fell to the concentrated ground fire.

During March and April 1945 the 386th and 391st Bomb Groups converted to the A-26 which when employed at medium altitude continued to do spectacular work to the end of the war.

In the Mediterranean Theatre the 47th Bombardment Group began receiving A-26s in January 1945. These aircraft were used primarily as night intruders. They were successful in destroying large numbers of enemy vehicles that had been forced to travel by night because of the ever present daylight fighter-bomber attacks.

Left: Until the A-26C with the glass bombardier nose came on the scene the A-20Js still had to lead the gun-nosed aircraft to the target. / *USAF*

Below left: An A-26 of the 386th Bomb Group in enemy flak. The speed of the Invader cut time over target down considerably to the gratification of the crews! / *USAF*

Right: Invaders of the 386th Bomb Group taxi out for a mission from their base in France. Operations on the Continent were usually off steel matting surface as illustrated here. / *USAF*

Below: *Stinky* of the 386th Group possessed the facial expression of a 'smiling shark'. / *USAF*

Above: One of the early A-26s sent to the Pacific for operations by the 3rd Bomb Group. The original closed-in type greenhouse cockpit was not liked in the Pacific. Note outboard wing gun pods.
/ T. K. Lewis

Below: *Winamac Werewolf* of the 416th Bomb Group gets airborne. Note the outboard wing gun pods on this A-26C. / USAF

In the summer of 1945 the 3rd Bombardment Group of the 5th Air Force in the Pacific began to receive B-26s once more. However, this time they were equipped with the new and improved canopy and were armed with eight .50 calibre machine guns in the nose and six internally mounted in the wings. The ventral turret had been removed to make room for additional fuel. This time the men of the 3rd were most enthusiastic about the aircraft and used them mixed in with their A-20s up to the end of the war. The last mission on which the A-26s participated in the 3rd Group took place on 12 August 1945. Fifteen Invaders joined 27 A-20s to drop incendiary bombs and napalm wing tanks on Kushikino, Kyushu Japan. The aircraft left their base on Okinawa and swept in over their target at low level. The first pass of the planes was made over an unburned part of the town. Six to eight large fires with smoke to 4,000ft and 20 smaller ones were started,

completely destroying this section of the town. Just south of the river a number of good sized fires were started. One bomb hit approximately 100 fuel drums in the dock area setting them afire and two napalm tanks hit a group of warehouse buildings and destroyed them. Approximately six fishing smacks in the southern breakwater were burnt out. In addition, the entire area was well strafed.

The 319th Bombardment Group which had been a Martin B-26 Marauder unit in the 12th Air Force returned to the United States in January 1945 to convert to A-26s. This unit

Above: French B-26C of GB 1/25 flying near Haiphong in early 1952 during the Indo-China conflict. / Cuny

Top right: Night fighter B-26 used by the French in North Africa to intercept light planes flown by the insurgents in Algeria in 1963. / Cuny

Bottom right: A formation of B-26Bs sets out on a daylight operation early in the Korean War. / McDonnell Douglas

was assigned to the 7th Air Force and entered combat flying the Invaders from Okinawa in July 1945. They flew their first mission on 16 July and dropped their bombs on an air-field on the Japanese home island of Kyushu. The 319th not only hit the Japanese homeland, they also flew missions against enemy bases in the vicinity of Shanghai, China.

One of their more outstanding missions took place on 10 August 1945. Thirty-one A-26s came in low-level waves over the factory centre of Kumamoto, Kyushu, fire bombing and strafing. Twenty-four tons of fire bombs were dropped on two large factory areas. As the Invaders left flames and des-truction behind them they sprayed the city with .50 calibre bullets as they raced for the coast at roof top level.

With the end of World War II the A-26s remained active in some light bomb and reconnaissance units of the USAAF while many of the aircraft were relegated to Air National Guard and Reserve units.

In January 1951 the French Armée de l'Air received the first of 111 Invaders which they employed in the war in Indo-China.

The French flew counter-insurgency attacks with the craft up to the cease fire in 1954 at which time 85 of the A-26s were returned to the USAF.

With the advent of the Korean conflict in June 1950 the A-26 (or B-26 as it had been redesignated by the USAF in 1947) was in on the first attack of the main North Korean airfield at Pyongyang on 29 June. Eighteen Invaders of the 3rd Bombardment Group succeeded in destroying 25 enemy aircraft on the ground and one of its gunners downed a Yak 3 that attempted an interception.

The 3rd was the only light bombardment unit available when the Korean conflict got under way and it had to hold the line alone until the arrival of the 452nd Bombardment Wing in October 1950. This unit was com-posed of reserve units which had been called to active duty and quickly went into combat. The 452nd flew its first combat mission on 27 October only 77 days after it had been called to active duty.

The two B-26 units did yeoman duty in ground support, flying both low and medium-level missions attacking enemy troop columns,

Top left: Detail shot showing the gun-nose of the B-26B to best advantage. These guns coupled with outboard wing pods gave the Invader tremendous fire power. / *USAF*

Left: Mixed formation of the 452nd Bomb Wing on their way to targets in Korea from their Japanese bases. The 452nd was composed of AF Reserve Squadrons which were rushed into combat in only 77 days. / *USAF*

Above: B-26s take-off from Japanese bases to strike at targets in Korea. Distance to the targets prevented the Invaders from carrying out their designed job in the early days of 1950. / *USAF*

Right: Invader carries a load of rockets to hit ground support targets in Korea. The B-26s ran the Communists off the road by day and had to begin night missions to cut the enemy transportation system. / *USAF*

motor transport and tanks. For medium level missions against bridges, road junctions and railway targets the units used their limited number of B-26Cs with glass bombardier noses to lead the missions for the hard-nosed B-26Bs. However, the gun-nosed pilots soon learned to make their own attacks using a combination of glide and dive bombing.

The B-26s left Japan in 1951, with the 452nd going to Pusan, Korea in May and the 3rd going to Kunsan in August. By this time most of their missions were being flown at night against rail and motor transport targets. This they fulfilled admirably. One innovation that was incorporated on some of the B-26s in the summer of 1951 was the installation of 80 million candlepower searchlights which could be used to illuminate the targets on the ground. However, this served more to illuminate the B-26 for ground fire than it did to the detriment of the enemy.

In May 1952 the 17th Bombardment Wing was activated to replace the reserve 452nd Wing as many of the men who had come to active duty with the unit had returned to the United States by this time. This did not change the operations, however, and the wing continued to fly their night intruder missions just as they had done before.

It was appropriate that the B-26s should fly the last combat mission of the Korean conflict on the evening of 27 July 1953 and that they should destroy the last enemy vehicle. A B-26 of the 17th Wing was credited with the vehicle and the 3rd Wing dropped the last bombs at 2136 hours.

Between 1950 and the end of the conflict in Algeria, the French operated a number of B-26s as counter-insurgency aircraft and modified a small number for use as night fighters.

The Invader was to see service in yet a third war with the USAF when Air Commando units employed the B-26 on counter-insurgency missions in Vietnam. At first the weary, unmodified aircraft were used, but as the war dragged on the B-26K was put into action. On-Mark Engineering Company all but rebuilt the aircraft. It was fitted with new R-2800-103-W engines equipped for water injection and developing 2,500hp. Wingtip fuel tanks were fitted for long range operations. Three .50 calibre machine guns were mounted in each wing and the aircraft nose fitting was optional. The gun nose housed eight .50 calibre machine guns and this could be easily changed for a glass nose for medium altitude bombing or reconnaissance operations.

Right: *Big Chief* a B-26 of the 13th Bomb Squadron, 3rd Bomb Wing, flew 215 combat hours in 30 consecutive days without any major maintenance. */ USAF*

Primarily used by the 606th Aero Commando Squadron flying from Nakhon Phanom Air Base in Thailand the B-26s did excellent night intruder work until they were finally retired from combat in 1969.

For a quarter of a century the Intruder performed nobly in a myriad of roles. It became a revered memory to many airmen who flew aboard in days of combat. It delighted many a pilot whose privilege it was to fly it and it left behind it a reputation of reliability and outstanding performance.

There are still a number of Invaders flying in civilian configuration and they promise to be around for some years to come. As one writer so aptly said of the aircraft, *'Old Invaders never die – they just keep on being reborn, and reborn, and . . .'*

Right: Cockpit of a B-26K. Note the optical head gunsight on the left. Engine instruments on the left, flight instruments on the right and armament switches across the top of the panel. / *J. Bardwell*

Below: An 'On Mark' B-26K in Vietnam. These highly modified Invaders were based in Thailand and used as counter insurgency aircraft with great effect. / *McDonnell Douglas*

A-26 Night Operations in Italy

The arrival of the A-26s brought about a new type of operation for the 86th Bombardment Squadron of the 47th Bombardment Group in Italy. The range and performance of the Invader made it an excellent intruder aircraft for nocturnal missions. This type of operation called for highly skilled crews with emphasis on those rare fliers who bore the title of bombardier-navigator. To carry out the intruder's job successfully it was essential that a crewman of this capability was on board.

Such a man was Lt Charles V. Wilson, bombardier-navigator, on one of the 86th Squadron's crews. As he relates his memories of those days:

'We had no particular assigned aircraft, but all were painted a flat matt black. A few of our aircraft carried .20mm cannon in the nose, but most of them were equipped with bombardier noses for missions such as those that I took part in. Our armament consisted of two .50 calibre machine guns in both the ventral and dorsal turrets operated by the gunner who rode in the rear of the Intruder. However, half the time we didn't even carry a gunner.

'Most of our missions were despatched to strike targets of opportunity. These usually were enemy airfields, bridges, marshalling yards and motor transport. On clear nights convoys could be sighted rolling along the highways.

'We had some real hot spots. In the area of Venice we could always expect searchlights and lots of flak. Flying at medium altitude,

Below: A B-26 revs up in preparation for heading out on a night mission against enemy transport. / USAF

80486A
G-131

113

10,000-14,000ft, you got a lot of firey tracers coming up.

'We usually travelled to the target by use of dead reckoning and then used the visual bombsight to good effect. We had a few missions where we were directed to targets that were covered by cloud. In these cases we used our ground radar stations to put us over the target and we bombed on their direction.

'Another type of bombing that we used was a combination of dive and glide bombing. We would sight a target from medium altitude and dive down to 3,000-4,000ft and make our run from the lower altitude. We very rarely used flares to illuminate our targets except after our bomb runs. Then we used the flares to see what damage we had done.

'About the only way we had to learn of enemy night fighters in the area was by monitoring the frequencies of the local RAF night fighter network. However, even when we knew that there were German night fighters in the area of our targets, there was little that we could do about them. In fact one of our greatest dangers was that of a mid-air collision with one of our own aircraft that was "free-lancing" in the same area.

'If we didn't find a target or had to abort we had a choice of bringing our bombs home or jettisoning them over the sea. We usually took the latter course of action for it was by far the safest!

'If we lost our radio or navigational aids, we were abetted in finding our course home by flare pots that would be lit at night in the mountains of northern Italy. These would serve to act as guides to get us back home to our base at Pisa. There were occasions when the Germans would also pass us false radio homings to lure us out over the sea to become lost and finally be forced to ditch. This may have well happened to some of our crews that never returned.'

The 47th proved that it was both a night and day unit during the period from 21 – 24 April 1945. The group maintained operations against the Germans for 60 consecutive hours, destroying enemy transport in the Po Valley to prevent the organised withdrawal of their forces. For this achievement, the 47th was awarded the Distinguished Unit Citation.

And just for the record one of the night raiders of the 47th was credited with a German night fighter. On the night of 20/21 March 1945, one of the A-26s engaged a German night fighter and in a running battle the gunner of the Intruder got in a scoring shot and the enemy exploded.

Below: Down the runway and away to strike at the German supply columns in Northern Italy is this A-26. / USAF

B-26s in Indo-China

Jean Cuny

'The first B-26s arrived in late 1950 and comprised about a third glass-nosed "leader" aircraft (B-26C), others being "Strafers" (B-26B) with either six guns or eight guns in solid noses. I never knew the exact number of delivered aircraft, but it probably came to about 25.

'The second batch came to Saigon during the end of 1951. It comprised only B-26Cs. Since they were equipped with wing twin-gun gondolas their users were quick to arm the planes as strafers, with two such gondolas under each wing. The aircraft used for precision bombing dispensed with fixed armament.

'I remember well a third batch of strafers arriving in mid-1953 and am told that there was a fourth batch delivered during Dien Bien Phu operations, but I can't verify this.

'Our basic mission was level bombing. The sighting was done from a "leader" nose, with Norden sight, and wingmen, normally "strafers" launched bombs on the leader. This was usually done by three-plane sections and before Dien Bien Phu, rarely more than three sections attacked a single target. Bombs were usually 500lb for buildings and dug-in targets, 250lb, 260lb anti-personnel fragmentation, and small anti-personnel bombs. Bombing altitudes were comprised between 1,000 and 5,000ft, the most common being 2,000ft during my period.

'Armed reconnaissances comprised the second main type of mission. We flew low

Below: A B-26B of GB 1/25 in 1953. Note the rocket mounts on the outboard wing sections and the absence of a ventral turret. / *Cuny*

and fast to shoot up any opportunity target. Generally these were flown in strafer type aircraft, but I did fly such missions carrying bombs. However, the latter had to be executed very rapidly before the enemy could disolve into the forest.

'With the war's progress the B-26s more often flew night missions, which were somewhat rare in the beginning. Of course then level bombing was normal, but I personally did reconnaissance, glide-bombing and even strafing at night during the Nghia-Lo/Na-San 1952 summer operations. During the Na-San siege there was very little margin for error for strikes were called in only 50yd from our trenches. The solution was obtained with an absolutely vertical light projector beam, used as a reference both for angular estimation of target position and for time-distance estimation (release time). The light was only in action when requested by the plane and it was inside a deep hole. Mortar fire could never destroy it.

'Our targets were static ones ie depots, communication lines, including bridges, trucks, etc. We could only rarely surprise and bomb infantry in action or displacement. Actually, during 18 months I only could really see the "Bo-Dois" twice during a bombing attack.

'Now, after discussing with surviving ground soldiers, I think our action was sometimes terrific, frequently annoying for the Viets, frequently unuseful, but this only because of intelligence or command inferiority.

'Crews were comprised of three men: pilot, navigator and gunner, who was simultaneously the flight engineer responsible for the aircraft. Less than a third of our navigators were bombardiers. There was a constant lack of Norden sight-qualified people. Most of our pilots had come from transport units or came from the old World War II bombing units which had operated on either Martin Marauder or Halifax bombers.

'The French pilots were high in their praise of the qualities of the B-26. Actually, for most of us, at least in the beginning, it was the first aircraft we had encountered which offered high manoeuvrability and excellent stability as a bombing or strafing platform. Several of my friends came out of dangerous situations thanks to the B-26's ability to do aerobatics.

'The aircraft was considered a "pilot's plane" with good controls and remarkable handling characteristics. It could accept heavy punishment. One of my wingmen did about 25 strafing passes during his return to base after cracking a main wing spar during a glide bombing attack. He heard the cracking but didn't believe it was "that important".'

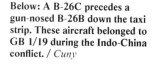

Below: A B-26C precedes a gun-nosed B-26B down the taxi strip. These aircraft belonged to GB 1/19 during the Indo-China conflict. / *Cuny*

Commander of the 3rd Bomb Wing

Maj Gen Nils Ohman

'When I took over the Third Bomb Wing in the spring of 1951, it was stationed at Iwakuni, Japan. It was equipped with two models of the Douglas B-26. The A-26B was a hard-nosed aircraft armed with eight .50 calibre guns in the nose and six .50 calibre machine guns mounted in the wings. This version had such terrific firepower that if all the guns were fired at one time it would nearly stall the aircraft.

'The Douglas A-26C had a glass nose and carried a bombardier. Armament consisted of six .50 calibre machine guns mounted in the wings.

'Both models of the B-26 were extremely solid and capable aircraft. The only drawback that we had to contend with in Japan was the fact that we were too far from the front. The range was just too extreme to make good use of the capability of the B-26. In August 1951, however, we moved to K-8, near Kunsan, Korea. This was an old US Army base and it had a number of permanent structures. Our move to western Korea had been pre-determined by higher headquarters.

'The 3rd Bomb Wing, was a regular Air Force organisation and my crews had a great deal of experience in flying the B-26s and it was decided that we would operate in western Korea where the land was flat that we could carry out low-level operations.

'The other B-26 wing in Korea, the 452nd, was made up of Air Force Reserve Squadrons just recently called to active duty. It was decided that they would operate in eastern Korea over the mountains and rugged country. There they would carry out medium altitude bombing operations.

Below: B-26C of the 3rd Bomb Wing flying off the cost of Korea in December 1953. / USAF

'Normally our operations got started just before dark. The crews had fixed routes that they flew to attack the enemy supply routes. Where possible we tried to keep the same crews flying the same routes. Soon they became so proficient that they could recognise any little differences which might indicate enemy operational buildups, even in the dark.

'The majority of our operations involved bombing and strafing enemy motor convoys and occasionally our aircraft would catch a train out in the open. On convoy strikes we normally tried to hit the front and then the rear of the column. Then the trucks in between could be destroyed at our leisure.

'In the summer of 1951 someone got the idea to hang searchlights on some of the B-26s in order to light up the targets at night. This served to illuminate the target alright, but it also made a prime target out of the aircraft carrying the searchlight. It was on such a mission that one of my pilots won the Medal of Honor, but died in the process.

'Capt John S. Walmsley was flying one of the searchlight-equipped aircraft on the evening of 14 September 1951. In the course of his operation he spotted and illuminated a train which he succeeded in disabling. Walmsley made attacking passes at the train until he exhausted his ammunition. He then radioed for other aircraft in the area to come in and complete its destruction. Upon the arrival of another B-26, Walmsley led the way in twice, illuminating the target with his searchlight. Unfortunately, Walmsley was taking a lot of anti-aircraft hits on his own aircraft while he made his attacks down the valley with the searchlight on. On the last pass he took a fatal hit and crashed into the side of a mountain and exploded.

'We also made a few daylight attacks during summer 1951, but most transportation targets took to hiding during the day and the attacks were not too successful.

'I took part in one attack in which I employed glide bombing techniques. When in the area of Wonsan I spotted a Russian built tank and destroyed it.

'One mission which stands out in my mind and further proved to me the capability of the B-26 was one in which I cornered five or six trucks on the road. I dropped flares for illumination and proceeded to strafe them with machine gun fire. On one pass I all but flew into a ridge. I heaved back on the yoke for all I was worth and know that I exceeded the stress rates for the aircraft, but it pulled out and held together. The trip back to base was uneventful.'

Left: Laden with bombs and rockets a flight of Invaders from the 3rd Bomb Wing head for a Communist target in North Korea in October 1952. / USAF

Below: Lineup of the 37th Bomb Squadron at K-1 in the autumn of 1952. The aircraft are armed for the night's mission. Squadron markings are in red. / *Mikesh*

Lt-Col Robert C. Mikesh (then Lt) was one of those pilots who flew the night interdiction missions in Korea. He put in his tour with the 17th Bomb Group during the period July to December 1952, flying from K-1 (Pusan West) and later from K-9. As Mikesh relates: 'Our 50 missions were not all the big explosions, trains off the track, etc, as some pilots would have you to believe.'

Theirs was a tour of little variance; most of the time they flew the same routes each mission. Once they learned the route they could spot any enemy activity almost at once, even in the moonlight. The usual bomb load was fragmentation bombs to be dropped on any behicles found on the road. Of course, the high spot was to catch a train but this did not happen too often, even in the course of 50 trips up over enemy territory.

One of his most memorable missions was his 33rd which took place on 22/23 October 1952. Here it is as he lived it:

'This, no doubt, will be the best mission that I will have flown in this tour of duty. I really had the feeling of satisfaction when it was over. I had a second "dollar rider", a pilot, Captain Prior along in the right seat and no doubt this impressed him also.

'The starting out of the mission wasn't too good, as I accidently inflated one chamber of my Mae West getting into the aircraft. Actually this was funny. The second thing was, after the engines were running while in the hard stand, we heard what sounded like a muffled explosion and felt a concussion. We couldn't figure out what it was. I had Kitchen (aerial gunner) look in the bomb bay from the rear compartment to see if we dropped a bomb on the doors, but negative report. I called runway control to come over and check the aircraft externally, but before he got there, I tried to look out the back, and found that my canopy was closed. What had happened was that the wind blew my canopy closed and that's what caused the concussion and noise. It's always a relief to find out what these things are as they worry a person throughout a flight unless they are explained, especially an explosive incident.

'Going inbound was uneventful. I told Marks (navigator/bombardier) that my missions were going by fast and that I wanted to claim the DFC for better than the six trucks we got the last time we were together. The guy took me seriously and did it!

'We found nothing at the road block so we went on to our assigned recce route. There weren't too many vehicles on it but enough that we didn't have to look too long to find something. Low clouds were hanging in a few of the valleys and trucks with their lights on, shining right through the clouds, probably thinking they were safe under them. They weren't this night and Marks was really hot.

'At no time did we drop more then two stations at a time and it seemed that everytime he did, we got secondary explosions! All colours ... The most explosions we got on any one attack was three and they totalled 14 in all, so he was really hitting them tonight. We made a total of 11 attacks of which only two had no visible results. Along with these 14 secondaries, which constituted claims for 14 trucks, we claimed two more due to two runs, there was one truck each between two close secondaries, and since the lights went out due to the explosions, they had to be destroyed by being that close.

'Again, I couldn't see what was going on, but from the large flashes that would occur, lighting up the cockpit, after the sparkle of the MIA2s going off, I could tell what was happening. My gunner, Kitchen, was in the waist compartment watching the whole show through the bomb bay. Each time we would light up the ground he would cut in with appropriate words of approval.

'Time went quickly and soon we were out of bombs so we headed for home. We were shot at with four 22mm guns on one run and four rounds from a "heavy" on another, but crossing south on the bomb line anymore seems to be the hardest job as they really open up. Just as we were crossing, all the heavy ground fire at the front which was just the last step to safety, heavy rounds began going off on both sides of the rear and closing in. That airplane was diving, turning and gaining airspeed all at one and yet we were having a hard time shaking it. They were really right on us. Soon we were out of range and heading for K-47, our first outbound check point south of the bomb line.'

Above: Pilot Bob Mikesh in the 'office' of his B-26 *Monie* which he flew in Korea. / *Mikesh*

Above right: Three-quarter rear view of *Monie* with photo flash bomb hung on the wing. This bomb was used for night photography in bomb damage assessment. / *Mikesh*

Right: Fine view of the nose of *Monie* which Mikesh named for his wife. This photo was taken in November of 1952 at K-1, Pusan West. The aircraft belonged to the 37th Bomb Squadron. / *Mikesh*

A Different War but the same Spirit

Nose art of B-26s in the Korean War. / *USAF, Mikesh, Rust and Liebold*

B-26 Navigator in Korea

Lt Charles Hinton

'I graduated from navigator training in November 1951 and instead of going to B-36s which had been my original assignment, I found myself, along with my entire class, on my way to Korea. Upon arrival I was assigned to the 13th Bombardment Squadron of the 3rd Bombardment Group. I discovered that my duties would entail low-level navigation in the course of primarily night interdiction missions aboard Douglas B-26Cs and Ds. I had not been trained for low-level navigation so it would be on the job training for me.

'At that time our group was composed of three squadrons each of which had eight B-26s. The mission load at that time called for approximately 44 sorties each night. This meant that one crew would go out, fly its mission and return in the early part of the night. The aircraft would be serviced, re-armed and a second crew would fly its mission.

'My first mission, or "dollar ride" as they were known for I had no responsibility as there was a veteran navigator aboard, was on 30 December 1951. We flew in a solid-nosed "D" model which had eight .50 calibre machine guns in the nose and three .50s in each wing. The navigator's post faced the tunnel going up to the nose and the wind always whined through the opening and there was never a mission that I wasn't cold. Fortunately, other than the cold the mission wasn't too bad and we returned to base with nothing spectacular to report.

'I was to find out what combat was all about on my third mission. This time I flew in a glass nosed "C" model with Lt "Cho-Cho" Baker who was flying his 55th and last mission before returning to the United States. He was called "Cho-Cho" because he was a locomotive ace. In our very unspectacular operations we got little publicity or glory, but the favourite targets of each and every pilot were locomotives and trains. Baker had destroyed over five locomotives during his tour so he was a locomotive ace.

'We were briefed to attack any vehicles on R-19 route which runs from Namchonjom through Sinmak to Sariwon. We took off at 2230 hours loaded with 3½ tons of bombs and .50 calibre ammo. We circled Namchonjom and then went down to 150-200ft for the run to the other end of the route. At that altitude and at 300mph we were almost impossible to hit. We gave Sinmak a wide berth because they threw everything at you. We came back on the road a little beyond Sinmak and went tooling down the track looking for a locomotive. We flew almost to Sariwon without sighting a thing and without being shot at.

'As we turned to head back our right engine surged up to almost twice its usual speed. We were still on the deck so Baker started to gain some altitude. An attempt to feather the propeller failed. We still couldn't gain any altitude so we salvoed the bombs.

'Baker cut the fuel to the engine so it wouldn't overheat and explode. By this time we had gotten up to approximately 3,000ft or nearly as high as the mountains around us. Baker called out a "Mayday", but we still figured we could get enough altitude to get home safely. The propeller was still windmilling and creating a lot of drag which caused us to lose altitude down to about 2,300ft. I saw a reflective glow on the back of the propeller and thought that the engine was on fire. We prepared to jump but decided to hold on a bit longer.

'Finally we began to gain a little altitude once more and our radar controller at Kimpo continued giving us directions. We were now down to about 150mph. We headed out over the water so we wouldn't jump over enemy held territory, but I had my doubts about that. The idea of coming down in icy water certainly was no attraction. Finally we got to within 30 miles of Kimpo and the fire came back – and much worse than before. I thought the plane would explode any instant but we couldn't jump.

'We came into Kimpo on a straight in approach. We got two green lights on the main gear but no light on the nose gear. There was no way we could go around so we continued our approach. Just as we flared out to touch down the third green light came on.

'An inspection of the aircraft on the ground showed that we had received a hit in the propeller dome from rifle fire. This caused the hydraulic fluid to leak out of the prop dome and caused the runaway. With all the flak we got shot at us we nearly bought it from a rifle shot!

'What was my most productive mission had nothing to do with our actual performance. On my 17th mission we created some explosions near Sinmak which we thought were vehicles, but we were suspicious enough to request that photos of the area be made. The photos showed that we had discovered a huge supply dump. A special mission by B-26s by night and F-80s by day destroyed one of the largest supply dumps ever discovered in Korea.'

Below: 3rd Bomb Wing Invaders head north in formation before breaking up to go their separate routes over North Korea. / *USAF*

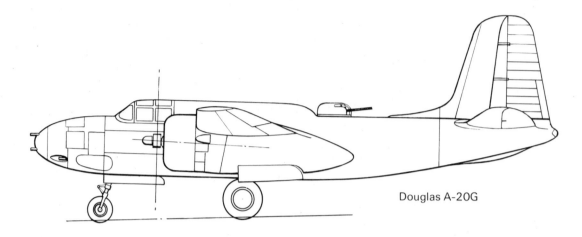

Douglas A-20G

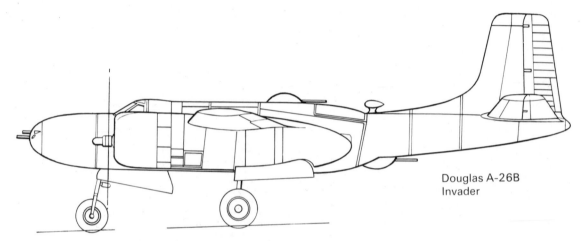

Douglas A-26B
Invader

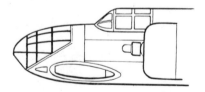

Nose of Douglas A-20C

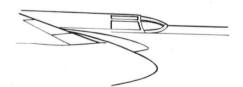

Rear gun position of
Douglas A-20C